From Kitchen to High Table
The British-American Edition

Copyright. 2005, 2008, 2012, Harris Manchester College
2012 O'More College of Design
2014 Hilliard Press

First published in 2005
Revised edition 2008
British-American Edition 2012

The right of David Woodfine to be identified as the author of this work has been asserted by him in accordance with the Copyright, Design and Patents Act 1988.

All rights reserved. No part of this publication may be reproduced, stored in a retrieval system, or transmitted, in any form or by any means, electronic, mechanical, photocopying, recording, or otherwise, without the prior permission of the publishers.

This book is sold subject to the condition that it shall not, by way of trade or otherwise, be lent, re-sold, hired out, or otherwise circulated without the publisher's prior consent in any form of binding or cover other than that in which it is published and without a similar condition including this condition being imposed on the subsequent purchaser.

Originally published by Harris Manchester College, Mansfield Road, Oxford OX1 3TD

ISBN 978-0-9555098-0-3

British-American Edition published by:
Hilliard Press
Franklin, TN 37067 U.S.A.

ISBN 978-0-9846244-6-1

Photography: Steve Harman
Illustrations: Sarah Keaggy
Book Design: Whitnee Webb
Cover Illustration: A watercolour of Harris Manchester College, Oxford, by Rod Warbrick

From Kitchen to High Table
The British-American Edition

by Dr. David Woodfine
Master Oxford City Guild of Chefs
High Steward (retired), Harris Manchester College,
Oxford University

www.hilliardpress.blogspot.com

FOREWORD

I was so very pleased when David asked me to write the foreword to accompany the cookery book he has compiled for Harris Manchester College.

David and I go back many years, and share a similar catering background, both being formally trained at catering colleges in the north of England, and gaining experience in the hotel and restaurant trade before entering the more formal and demanding world of private service, where standards and attention to detail are paramount.

Although never having the opportunity to work at colleges in Oxford, I know of their remarkably high standard in both kitchen and dining room, and can see a clear similarity with private service, where both traditions and good kitchen practice are maintained.

Sadly, the modern image of a working kitchen today appears to be one of intimidation, bad language, and lack of respect shown towards the young people you are responsible for encouraging.

This book contains many valued traditional dishes, sitting comfortably alongside their more modern counterparts that now excite the palate. It will be a useful and informative addition to the domestic kitchen, and a great contribution to the cookery books in the kitchen office, where it will be referred to frequently for both recipes and inspiration.

With my highest recommendation,

M H Adams *(Personal Chef to Lord Rothschild)*
1985-1989 Head Chef to the Marquis and Marchioness of Tavistock
1982-1985 Head Chef to the Duke and Duchess of Westminster
1969-1982 Head Chef to the Duke and Duchess of Marlborough

DAVID WOODFINE
HIS STORY
By Dr. K. Mark Hilliard

I first met David Woodfine during the summer of 2007 when I was a part of the Oxford Roundtable at Jesus College, University of Oxford, England. I was presenting a paper on the Art and Science of Teaching and Learning to a group of professors and academic leaders from all over the world and experiencing Oxford for the first time. During a tour of several of the other Colleges of Oxford University, I was blessed to visit Harris Manchester. While there I met David, purchased an original version of his book, *From Kitchen to High Table*, and learned about the Harris Manchester Summer Research Institute. I have since spent parts of three summers at Harris Manchester conducting research for my own books and getting to know David and more about his exciting life experiences. I will share a part of David's story below, and I hope you enjoy this special version of his wonderful book, *From Kitchen to High Table, The British–American Edition*, published once by O'More Publishing and now Hilliard Press.

In his early career, David Woodfine trained and served as a chef and catering manager, including two years as head chef at the Moorcock Inn, Waddington, and two years as head chef at the Calf Head Hotel, Clitheroe. He then moved into catering management and has continued for the last fifty years in key roles throughout England within the catering and hospitality industry. He retired from full-time employment in June 2011.

David also served his country, spending eleven years with

the Territorial Army (Britain's Reserve Land Forces) as a Regular Reserve, providing support at home and overseas. His responsibilities included working "in the field," often cooking for more than 250 soldiers and officers, and overseeing the preparation and service of multiple regimental dinners.

During the past thirty-plus years, David has been a Lecturer for the Business and Technology Education Council (B.T.E.C.) in Hotel and Catering Management, for the City and Guilds (C & G) Level 1 Food Service, and for the Wine and Spirit Education Trust Higher Certificate.

To widen his experience, David left his home in England for a while and was employed as a butler at various places throughout Europe. In this role he served highly respected dignitaries and was fortunate to have tea with Kings and Queens.

On returning to England, David became the butler to Sir Anthony and Lady Bamford (founders of the world famous JCB Diggers/Excavators) and Mr. and Mrs. Richard Hambro (well known in the world of corporate finance as well as the breeding and racing of horses, with a personally owned stud farm in Gloucestershire, England). The Bamfords' main residences in England are a 1500 acre estate in the Cotswolds, a 3000 acre estate at Wotton in Staffordshire, homes in Chelsea, London, and also homes in France and Barbados.

David was also a butler to His Grace The Duke of Marlborough at Blenheim Palace. Blenheim Palace is in Woodstock, near Oxford, and was built, on Queen Anne's orders, for John Churchill, the 1st Duke of Marlborough, in recognition of his victory at the Battle of Blenheim in 1704—a victory that saved Europe from French domination. The property has 2100 acres of landscaped parkland designed by 'Capability' Brown. Sir Winston Churchill was born in Blenheim Palace and the current Duke, for whom David was butler, is the 11th Duke of Marlborough. David was involved in the running of the household and various private events hosted by the Duke and Duchess that included shooting parties and caring for royal and notable dignitaries visiting from around the world.

In his role as butler, David often looked after royalty including His Royal Highness The Prince of Wales and Her Royal Highness The Princess of Wales, as well as multiple European Heads of State. Her Royal Highness Princess Margaret was always a favourite guest of David's at Blenheim, as was the actress Joan Collins.

More recently, David was the High Steward at Harris Manchester College, University of Oxford. He provided pastoral care and the highest quality of hospitality to the students, faculty, guests, donors, and corporate clients. David has a passion for hosting weddings and other grand events, the most notable being the wedding of Lord Andrew Lloyd Webber.

Upon his retirement from Harris Manchester in 2011, David became the Master of the Oxford City Guild of Chefs. In this role, David oversees the organization of multiple Oxford University College dinners with Oxford's top chefs. The position also involves mentoring young people who are entering this industry.

From Kitchen to High Table is a collection of David's recipes and details about British formal dining etiquette. The High Table, in a College setting, is usually situated on the stage or on a raised platform in the main dining hall. Seated at this table during a formal affair are the Principal of the College (similar to a university president in the United States), its tutors (in the United States this would be the professors or teachers), distinguished guests, and visiting dignitaries. The responsibility for this formal event, from what happens in the kitchen to what happens at the High Table, belongs to the High Steward. This sophisticated choreography of preparation, oversight, and follow-through is David Woodfine's forte.

I hope you enjoy this book and take the time to prepare many of the delightful recipes David has shared with us. While at Harris Manchester College, I experienced many lovely evenings orchestrated by David. Some took place at the High Table, but many were simply shared on the beautiful campus green amongst a group of academics talking about teaching and learning, with David Woodfine as our host.

Dr. K. Mark Hilliard
Director General, Oxford Centre
of the Study of Law and Public Policy
Visiting Fellow, Harris Manchester College, Oxford University

HARRIS MANCHESTER COLLEGE, OXFORD UNIVERSITY

Harris Manchester College was originally founded as the Warrington Academy in 1757.

The College was re-founded in Manchester, England, in 1786 to train people for the learned professions and civil and commercial life. John Dalton, famous for his atomic theory, was appointed a Professor of the College in 1793. Early teaching staff also included James Martineau, the Victorian theologian and philosopher. The college was one of the last of a long line of 'dissenting academies' established after the Restoration to provide higher education for Nonconformists.

In 1840 the College received a Royal Letter in Council signed by Queen Victoria, making it a Collegiate Society of the University of London, with the same status as University College and King's College.

In 1889, following an act of Parliament that abolished religious tests at Oxford, Cambridge, and Durham Universities, the College moved to Oxford as a permanent private hall with the intention of joining the University of Oxford. It was not until 1990 that the College became a full college of the University of Oxford. The College was granted a Royal Charter, making it the thirty-ninth College of the University of Oxford, and, following a generous benefaction from Lord Harris and his family, it became known as Harris Manchester College. Harris Manchester College is now the thirty-seventh College of the University of Oxford following the merger of Templeton College and Green College.

Harris Manchester College is a non-traditional College, only accepting students over the age of twenty-one to study for Oxford first degrees and higher degrees. The College is small and friendly with approximately one hundred undergraduates, fifty postgraduates (including fourteen medical students) and sixty students reading for the Oxford Doctorate in Clinical Psychology.

http://www.hmc.ox.ac.uk

ACKNOWLEDGEMENTS

I should like to thank the Revd Dr Ralph Waller, Principal of Harris Manchester College, University of Oxford, for giving me the time and support to produce this cookery book. I am also very grateful to Michael Adams for agreeing to write the foreword. My thanks go to Elizabeth Machin and Amanda Carpenter, who typed the original version of this book, and to Whitnee Webb, the Creative Director from O'More College of Design in Franklin, Tennessee, USA, who designed this special British-American Edition. Everything on the inside of this book was laid out, including photography, illustrations, and all the design elements, by Ms Webb.

My gratitude goes to Karol Lahrman, Reflection Talent and Model Agency, USA, for overseeing the newly added Dining Etiquette section of the book; to Steve Harman for his beautiful photography of my recipes; to Judy and Will Matheny, O'More Chefs and owners of Providence Farms Foods, who prepared the recipes photographed for this book; to Sarah Keaggy for her lovely Dining Etiquette illustrations; to our wonderful editors, Rosemary J. Hilliard, Lindsay Hines, and Judy and Will Matheny; and to the former Executive Editor of O'More Publishing and current owner of Hilliard Press, Professor Jessa R. Sexton.

The proposal to create this British-American Edition was the initiative of Dr K. Mark Hilliard, who graciously oversaw the development of this project and published this unique version. Finally, I should like to thank Sue Killoran, Fellow Librarian at Harris Manchester College, for her support, proofreading, and advice throughout the entire process of my first and second editions, as well as this British-American edition.

David Woodfine

Table of Contents

COCKTAILS 14

SOUPS 20

STARTERS 28

FISH 36

MEAT & POULTRY 48

EGGS 74

SAVOURIES 84

PUDDINGS 100

CAKES 134

BISCUITS & SCONES 152

JAMS & MARMALADES 158

VEGETARIAN 164

DINING ETIQUETTE 180

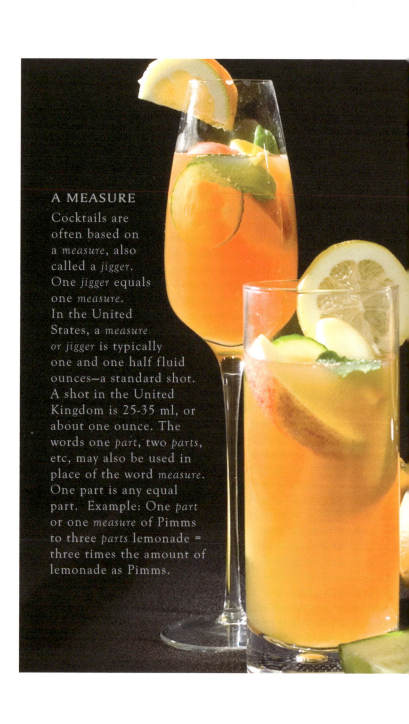

A MEASURE

Cocktails are often based on a *measure*, also called a *jigger*. One *jigger* equals one *measure*. In the United States, a *measure* or *jigger* is typically one and one half fluid ounces—a standard shot. A shot in the United Kingdom is 25-35 ml, or about one ounce. The words one *part*, two *parts*, etc, may also be used in place of the word *measure*. One part is any equal part. Example: One *part* or one *measure* of Pimms to three *parts* lemonade = three times the amount of lemonade as Pimms.

COCKTAILS

Pimms No. 1 Cocktail

Pimms No. 1 Cocktail

INGREDIENTS

Pimms No. 1 (bottled alcoholic drink)
Lemonade
Mint sprigs
Cucumbers
Lemons
Oranges
Apples (or other fresh fruit as desired)

METHOD

1. In a tall glass, mix one measure or part of Pimms to three measures or parts of lemonade.
2. Add a slice of cucumber, lemon, orange, apple, or other fruit as desired, and a sprig of mint. These ingredients may also be cubed.

Pimms No. 1 is a proprietary mixture that is blended with lemonade and decorated with mint, cucumber, lemon, orange, or other fresh fruit such as apple, strawberry, etc. It is a lovely British pre-dinner cocktail for a warm summer day. The original recipe for Pimms is a secret, but it is based on gin and can be traced back to the early 1800s when its creator (James Pimm, from London) used gin, quinine, and a variety of herbs to make his now famous drink. Pimms No. 1 is the most famous Pimms mix but there were also a variety of other Pimms recipes (No. 2 - 6) created after World War II, that used scotch, brandy, rum, rye, and vodka, respectively.

Buck Fizz (or Buck's Fizz)

INGREDIENTS

Chilled champagne
Orange juice
Orange wedges or slices

METHOD

1. In a champagne flute, mix two measures of fresh orange juice to one measure chilled champagne.
2. Add an orange wedge to garnish.

Buck's Fizz is named after the Buck's Club, a gentleman's club in London dating back to the early 1900s, where the cocktail was first created. The original recipe is two parts orange juice and one part chilled champagne, garnished with an orange wedge. The Mimosa, created in Paris, usually contains equal parts of orange juice and champagne or sparkling wine.

Champagne Cocktail

The Champagne Cocktail is a poured cocktail, served in a champagne flute or goblet.

INGREDIENTS

Chilled champagne
Brandy
Sugar cubes or lumps
Angostura bitters
Orange wedges or slices

METHOD

1. One lump of sugar is placed in the glass and saturated with Angostura bitters (just a dash or two).
2. Add a small amount of brandy ($\frac{1}{3}$ oz or so), and top up with chilled champagne.
3. Add a slice of orange and serve.

Champagne cocktails can be traced back to the 1800s, with recipes from all over the world.

Kir Royal

INGREDIENTS

Crème de cassis (black currant liqueur)
Chilled champagne

METHOD

1. Pour one half measure of crème de cassis in a champagne flute.
2. Top up with chilled champagne poured slowly over the crème de cassis. (It mixes much better if you add the champagne to the crème de cassis.)

The history of the Kir Royal is a mix of fact and myth. What is known is that the name relates to a priest and hero of the French Resistance during World War II. Canon Félix Kir was from the northern French province of Burgundy and became the mayor of Dijon in the mid 20th Century. Kir, without the Royal name added to its title, refers to the drink's original mix, using white wine instead of champagne. One story goes that the addition of the black currant liqueur, known as crème de cassis, made very cheap wine more palatable and therefore more marketable. Later on, the name Kir Royal came to be when those of royal background began to substitute champagne for the white wine. Though difficult to determine where the fact and myth starts and ends with this story, you are sure to enjoy the product, no matter its history.

SOUPS

Tomato and Dill Bisque

Tomato and Dill Bisque

INGREDIENTS

Serves 4-6

900g (2 lbs) fresh tomatoes
1 onion, peeled and chopped
2 large sprigs fresh dill
30ml (2 Tbsp) tomato paste
Salt and freshly ground black pepper
850ml (3½ cups) vegetable stock
140ml (⅔ cup) double cream (whipping cream)
10ml (2 tsp) chopped fresh dill
60ml (¼ cup) natural yogurt
4 slices tomato
4 small sprigs fresh dill

METHOD (MICROWAVE RECIPE)

1. Cut the tomatoes in half over a bowl and remove the seeds. Reserve any juice that is produced.
2. Put the tomato flesh and any juice into a large bowl along with the onion, 2 dill sprigs, tomato paste, salt, pepper, and vegetable stock.
3. Partially cover the bowl with cling film.
4. Cook in the mircrowave on high for 7 minutes, or until the tomatoes have broken down and the onions are soft.
5. Remove the sprigs of dill and, using a liquidiser or food processor, purée the soup until it is smooth.
6. Strain the puréed soup back into the bowl through a metal sieve to remove the tomato skins.
7. Stir the double cream and chopped dill into the puréed tomato soup and mix well.
8. Cook on high for 30 seconds to reheat.
9. Garnish each serving with a spoonful of the yogurt, a tomato slice, and a sprig of dill before serving.

Basic Lettuce Soup...Plus

INGREDIENTS

Serves 4-6

>1 large onion, chopped
>Oil
>Outside leaves and stalks of lettuce
>   (the more you have, the tastier it gets)
>900ml (4 cups) chicken stock
>50g (2oz) peas
>Freshly ground black pepper
>Sugar

METHOD

1. Fry the onion lightly in a little oil.
2. Shred the lettuce leaves, add them to the pan and fry on for a few minutes; pour in chicken stock and add peas.
3. Season with pepper and a pinch of sugar and simmer gently for half an hour.
4. Pour into a liquidiser and whizz to a pulp.
5. When you have puréed, return to pan. Heat up for 5 minutes and serve.
6. If you make this soup in the summer, you can add sorrel, lemon balm, tarragon, chives, watercress leaves, or any complementary herb.

Homemade soups are one of the best value-for-money foods going. You can add almost anything you've got, and every time you make some the mixture is different.

Parsnip and Apple Soup

Rich, thick, and creamy.

INGREDIENTS
Serves 4

25g (2 Tbsp) butter
700g (½ lb) parsnips, peeled and roughly chopped
1 Bramley (tart) cooking apple, cored, peeled,
 and roughly chopped
1.1l (4⅔ cups) chicken stock
4 fresh sage leaves or 2ml (½ tsp) dried sage
2 whole cloves
150ml (⅔ cup) fresh single cream (half and half)
Salt and freshly ground black pepper
Fresh sage leaves or parsley and croutons to garnish

METHOD

1. Melt the butter in a large pan. Add the parsnips and apple. Cover and simmer for 10 minutes, stirring occasionally.
2. Pour in the stock; add the sage leaves and cloves. Bring to the boil, cover and simmer for 30 minutes or until the parsnips are tender.
3. Remove the sage leaves and cloves. Leave to cool slightly, then purée in a blender or food processor.
4. Return to the pan and reheat gently with the cream. Season to taste.
5. Serve hot, garnished with sage or parsley and croutons.

French Onion Soup

Rich and brown with lots of onions and cheesy hunks of bread, this soup is deliciously filling as a lunch time snack or as a starter for a dinner.

INGREDIENTS

Serves 4

15ml (1 Tbsp) oil
40g (3 Tbsp) butter
10ml (2 tsp) dark brown sugar
450g (1 lb) onions, peeled and sliced
1.2l (5 cups) beef stock
6 slices French bread
Gruyere cheese, grated

METHOD

1. Heat oil and butter in a pan. Add onions and sugar, stir until brown. Cover and cook over low heat until the onions are soft, about 10-12 minutes.
2. Add boiling stock and seasoning. Simmer gently, covered, for 20-30 minutes.
3. Slice French loaf, cover with grated cheese and grill (broil). Serve floating on the soup.

Minestrone Special Soup

There's nothing as hearty and warming as a homemade soup to take the chill out of winter.

INGREDIENTS
Serves 4-6

25g (2 Tbsp) butter
30ml (2 Tbsp) olive oil
1-2 sticks celery, chopped
1 large carrot, peeled and chopped
1-2 onions, peeled and chopped
1 small turnip, peeled and chopped
1 potato, peeled and chopped
1 clove garlic, peeled and crushed
850ml (4 cups) good beef stock
2 large tomatoes
2 green peppers, de-seeded and chopped
1 leek, sliced
½ white cabbage, sliced
25g (¼ cup) macaroni
Salt and pepper to taste

METHOD

1. Heat butter and oil in a large pan and add celery, carrot, onion, turnip, and potato together with crushed garlic. Sauté for a few minutes, then add hot stock. Cover pan and simmer for 15 minutes or until vegetables are almost tender.
2. Halve the tomatoes, remove seeds and chop flesh. Add to the pan with peppers, leek, and cabbage. Bring back to the boil.
3. Add pasta and simmer without lid for 10-15 minutes.
4. Season.

STARTERS

Potato Pancakes with Caviar

Potato Pancakes with Caviar

There's something wonderfully extravagant about putting caviar on an earthy potato pancake. These need to be sautéed the minute before they're eaten, so I make them when we're all cooking together. Then we have something special to eat while we're getting dinner ready.

INGREDIENTS
Serves 6-8

4 large baking potatoes
2 extra-large eggs, whisked
84g (¾ cup) all-purpose flour
12ml (2½ tsp) salt
2ml (½ tsp) freshly ground pepper
84g (6 Tbsp) clarified butter (see note)
119ml (½ cup) cup crème fraîche or sour cream
2oz good caviar or salmon roe

METHOD

1. Peel the potatoes and grate them lengthwise. Place them in a colander or kitchen towel and squeeze out as much liquid as possible.
2. Combine the potatoes in a bowl with the eggs, flour, salt, and pepper. Mix well.
3. Melt 2 Tbsp of the clarified butter in a skillet over medium heat. Drop a Tbsp of the potato mixture into the sizzling butter. Flatten with a spatula and cook for 2 minutes. Turn, flatten again, and cook for another 2 minutes, or until crisp on the outside and golden brown.
4. Serve the pancakes hot from the skillet with a dollop of crème fraîche and a tsp of caviar.

To make 6 Tbsp clarified butter, slowly melt 8 Tbsp butter in a small saucepan. Set it aside until the milk solids settle. Spoon off any solids that rise, then carefully pour off the golden liquid, discarding the milky part in the bottom of the pan.

Chicken Liver Parfait

INGREDIENTS

Serves 4-6

225g (½ lb) chicken livers
Salt and black pepper
110g (½ cup) butter
20g-30g (1½-2 Tbsp) brandy
20g-30g (1½-2 Tbsp) dry sherry
120ml (½ cup) double cream (whipping cream), chilled

METHOD

1. Thoroughly clean the chicken livers, removing every trace of staining from the gall bladders, which would make the dish bitter, and all stringy bits.
2. Season the livers generously with salt and pepper.
3. Melt the butter in a saucepan and add the livers. Cook, uncovered, at the gentlest of simmers for 10-15 minutes, so that the livers are cooked through but not toughened.
4. Remove the pan from the heat and set aside until cool, then chop or process the livers with the butter and work the mixture through a fine sieve.
5. Beat in the brandy and sherry and set the bowl on crushed ice in a larger bowl.
6. Whip the cream until it holds soft peaks. Working over the ice, beat it into the liver mixture, a spoonful at a time.
7. Check the seasoning and divide the parfait between small individual serving dishes or spoon it into one larger dish.
8. Cover and chill until needed.
9. Serve with crusty bread or toast.

Duck Terrine with Orange

INGREDIENTS
Serves 4-6

2kg (4½ lbs) oven-ready duck
450g (1 lb) belly pork (bacon)
225g (½ lb) pork fat
1 orange
225g (½ lb) onions, peeled and finely chopped
1 clove garlic, crushed
60ml (¼ cup) red wine
30ml (2 Tbsp) chopped parsley
5ml (1 tsp) ground mace
5ml (1 tsp) salt
Pinch of pepper
1 orange for garnish

METHOD

1. Cut away the skin and fat layer from the duck and remove the flesh, about 700g.
2. Remove the rind from the belly pork.
3. Pass all the meat and pork fat twice through a fine mincer.
4. Grate the rind from the orange.
5. Remove all pith and membrane, collecting any juice, and cut the flesh into small dice.
6. Combine the minced meats, orange rind, chopped orange and any juice, and all remaining ingredients except the garnish.
7. Press the pâté into an earthenware terrine, pie, or soufflé dish.
8. Cover with foil. Put in a moderate oven, 180°C (350°F), Gas mark 4, for about 3 hours.
9. Strain off the juices and skim off the surface fat.

Duck Terrine with Orange

CONTINUED

10. Reduce these to a glaze and pour the juices over the pâté.
11. Cover and weight down.
12. Refrigerate until cold.
13. Unmold onto a serving platter.
14. Peel the remaining orange, slice it thinly and use half slices to garnish the dish.

Mushroom Florentine

INGREDIENTS
Serves 4

900g (2 lbs) fresh spinach, washed
105g (½ cup) butter, divided
450g (1 lb) open cap mushrooms
2 shallots, finely chopped
4 tomatoes, peeled, seeded, and chopped
Salt and freshly ground pepper
Pinch of nutmeg
45g (⅓ cup) plain flour
20ml (4 tsp) dry mustard powder
Pinch of cayenne pepper
570ml (2¼ cups) milk
225g (2 cups or ½ lb) Cheddar cheese, grated
Paprika for garnish

METHOD (MICROWAVE RECIPE)

1. Put the spinach into a large bowl with a pinch of salt. Cover the bowl with cling film and pierce this several times with the tip of a sharp knife.
2. Cook the spinach for 4 minutes on high. Leave to stand until required.
3. Put 60g (4 Tbsp) of butter into a large bowl, cook on high for 30 seconds to melt.
4. Wash the mushrooms, peel off any tough outer skin, and trim the stalks with a sharp knife.
5. Add the mushrooms to the melted butter and stir well to coat them evenly. Cook for 3 minutes on high, stirring after each minute of cooking time.
6. Remove the mushrooms from the bowl with a slotted spoon, draining off as much cooking liquid as possible, setting them to one side on a plate.
7. Stir the shallots into the mushroom juices and cook on high for 2 minutes, stirring once during the cooking time.
8. Drain the spinach and shred it roughly.

Mushroom Florentine

CONTINUED

9. Add the shredded spinach to the cooked shallots, along with the tomatoes, seasoning, and nutmeg. Stir well to mix evenly.
10. Spread the spinach mixture evenly over the bottom of a large casserole dish. Arrange the mushrooms over the top.
11. Melt the remaining butter in a deep bowl on high for 1 minute.
12. Stir in the flour, mustard, seasoning, and cayenne pepper, blending thoroughly with a wooden spoon to form a roux.
13. Gradually add the milk to the flour paste, beating thoroughly and cooking, uncovered, for 30 seconds between additions.
14. Whisk the sauce until it is smooth, then stir in 180g (1½ cups) of cheese. Heat on high for 1 minute to melt the cheese.
15. Pour the sauce over the mushrooms and sprinkle the remaining cheese and the paprika evenly over the top.

FISH

Tuna Steak with Wine and Bacon

Tuna Steak with Wine and Bacon

INGREDIENTS
Serves 4

>15ml (1 Tbsp) olive oil
>125g (¼ lb) bacon, coarsely chopped
>2 onions, sliced
>750g (1⅔ lb) fresh tuna,
>   cut into steaks 3cm (1¼ inch) thick
>230ml (1 cup) dry white wine
>Salt and black pepper

METHOD

1. Heat the oil in a frying pan and fry the bacon and onions until the onions are soft and the bacon starts to brown.
2. Add the tuna and lightly fry on both sides. Pour in the wine and simmer over a low heat for 10 minutes.
3. Season and serve with the bacon, onions, and cooking juice over the tuna.

Moules Marinière

INGREDIENTS

Serves 4-6

> 30g (2 Tbsp) butter
> 15g (2 Tbsp) flour
> 1kg (2.2 lbs) mussels
> 30g (2 Tbsp) finely chopped shallots
> 62ml (¼ cup) dry white wine
> 62ml (¼ cup) fish stock juice
> 68ml (⅓ cup) cream
> 15g (1 Tbsp) butter
> Salt and pepper
> ½ lemon, juiced
> Cayenne pepper, to taste

METHOD

1. Mix together flour and butter.
2. Wash and scrape the mussels well.
3. Place in a large pan with the shallots, wine, and fish stock.
4. Cook quickly under cover for 5 minutes.
5. Remove mussels, take off beards, and half the shell.
6. Place in a casserole to keep warm.
7. Decant and strain the cooking liquor to a clean pan and reduce by half with a little cream.
8. Thicken slightly with butter and flour you have mixed together, and enrich the sauce with a little butter. Season; add lemon juice and cayenne pepper.
9. Pour the sauce over the mussels.

Poached Smoked Haddock

INGREDIENTS

Serves 4

4 fillets of smoked haddock
30g (2 Tbsp) butter
300ml (1¼ cups) milk
Salt and black pepper

METHOD

1. Melt butter in a large saucepan. Place fish in the saucepan.
2. Cover with milk and sprinkle with salt and black pepper.
3. Simmer gently for 10-15 minutes or until tender.
4. Remove from pan and place on a serving dish.

The haddock can be served topped with a poached egg.

Smoked Haddock Kedgeree

*A dish of Anglo-Indian origin,
consisting of rice, cooked fish, and hard-boiled eggs.*

INGREDIENTS

Serves 4

> 450g (1 lb) smoked haddock
> 175g (1 cup) long grain rice
> 2 or 3 hard-boiled eggs
> 75g (⅓ cup) butter
> Salt
> Cayenne pepper
> Chopped parsley

METHOD

1. Cook and flake the fish.
2. Cook the rice in the usual way and drain if necessary.
3. Shell the eggs. Chop one and slice the others into rings.
4. Melt the butter in a saucepan. Add the fish, rice, chopped eggs, salt, and cayenne pepper and stir over a moderate heat for about 5 minutes until hot.
5. Pile it on a hot dish and garnish with lines of chopped parsley and the sliced egg. Serve with green salad.

Breakfast Kedgeree

Smoked Haddock, especially from Scotland and Findon, a small village near Aberdeen, has given its name to the very delicious creamy-yellow Smoked Finnan haddies that are produced there.

INGREDIENTS
Serves 4

225g (1¼ cups) long grain rice
50g (¼ cup) butter
3 eggs, hard boiled
450g (1 lb) smoked haddock, cooked and flaked
Salt and pepper
Chopped parsley

METHOD

1. Cook the rice in the usual way and drain if neccesary.
2. Melt the butter in a pan. Add the rice, roughly chopped hard boiled eggs, and flaked smoked haddock.
3. Season to taste and cook over a gentle heat until the ingredients are thoroughly heated.
4. Pour into a hot serving dish and garnish with the chopped parsley.

Smoked haddock makes a good breakfast, lunch, or tea dish and an excellent kedgeree and other savouries such as fish soufflé.

Smoked Haddock Soufflé

INGREDIENTS
Serves 4-6

225g (½ lb) smoked haddock
28g (2 Tbsp) cornflour (cornstarch)
300ml (1¼ cups) milk
30g (2 Tbsp) butter
75g (⅔ cup) cheese, grated
1-2 eggs, separated
Salt and pepper

METHOD

1. Grease a 1 litre (2 pint) ovenproof dish.
2. Cook and flake the fish.
3. Blend the cornflour with 15 ml (2 Tbsp) of the cold milk. Boil the remainder of the milk with the butter. Pour on to the blended cornflour, stirring well.
4. Return the mixture to the pan and heat until boiling, stirring until the sauce thickens.
5. Remove from the heat. Add the cheese, fish, and egg yolks and season well.
6. Whisk the egg whites stiffly and fold into the fish mixture.
7. Pour in the dish and bake in a moderately hot oven, 200°C (400°F), Gas mark 6, for about 20 minutes, until well risen and golden.
8. Serve immediately, because the mixture sinks as it cools.

Smoked Trout or Salmon Pate

INGREDIENTS
Serves 4-6

225g (½ lb) smoked trout or salmon
50g (¼ cup) butter
75g (½ cup) fresh white breadcrumbs
Finely grated rind and juice of 1 lemon
Salt and freshly ground black pepper
Pinch nutmeg
150ml (⅔ cup) single cream (half and half)
150ml (⅔ cup) aspic jelly

METHOD

1. Finely chop the flesh of smoked trout or salmon.
2. Melt butter in a small pan and pour it onto the breadcrumbs with the lemon rind and juice.
3. Season well with salt, pepper, and nutmeg.
4. Add the fish to the breadcrumbs and fold the cream through.
5. Spoon the mixture into 6 ramekins.
6. Make up the aspic jelly and when it is on the point of setting, spoon it over the fish mixture. (For aspic jelly-use leaf gelatine or 1 Tbsp of aspic jelly powder. Aspic jelly powder needs to be mixed with cold fish stock and then gently heated and allowed to cool, then it is ready to be used...but don't allow it to set before you use it. If you use leaf gelatine, just follow the instructions on the packet.)
7. Chill the pate and serve with hot buttered toast.

Salmon Fish Cakes

INGREDIENTS

Serves 4-6

450g (1 lb) potatoes, peeled and quartered
30ml (2 Tbsp) tomato ketchup
5ml (1 tsp) English mustard
Salt and freshly ground black pepper
2 fresh salmon fillets, steamed and flaked
45ml (3 Tbsp) sunflower oil

METHOD

1. Place the potatoes in a pan with just enough water to cover. Bring to the boil, cover and simmer for 15-20 minutes, or until tender. Drain well and mash.
2. Stir the ketchup, mustard, seasoning, and half the salmon into the mash and mix well until smooth. Gently stir in the remaining salmon, cover and chill.
3. When chilled, shape into 6 evenly sized fish cakes.
4. Heat the oil in a pan and fry the fish cakes over a medium heat for 10-15 minutes, turning half way through, until golden brown and piping hot.

Serve hot with buttered spinach.

Salmon Fried with Lemon

INGREDIENTS
Serves 6

750g (1⅔ lb) salmon or salmon trout
5ml (1 tsp) salt
Oil or butter
2 lemons
2 small cucumbers about 13cm (5 inch) long

METHOD

1. Cut the salmon into six steaks, across the body.
2. Sprinkle with salt and let stand for several minutes. Rinse off and wipe dry.
3. In a heavy-based frying pan, heat the oil or butter. Fry the fish gently for 4 minutes on each side.
4. Sprinkle with juice of 1 lemon during cooking.
5. When the fish is cooked, lift each slice onto a small plate, preferably rectangular, and decorate with cucumber fans and lemon butterflies prepared as follows:
6. Wash the cucumbers and cut each into 3 pieces.
7. Slice each piece lengthwise into 5mm (¼ inch) slices, discarding the end pieces.
8. To make cucumber fans, use a very sharp knife to cut each slice into strips, leaving the end 5mm (¼ inch) uncut. Gently press the 'fan' ribs open.
9. Slice the remaining lemon into thin slices and make butterfly shapes by cutting away a small triangle from two opposite sides, leaving wing-like shapes.

Fried Fish in Beer Batter

INGREDIENTS

Serves 6

6 large fish or 12 small fillets
Juice of lemon
Salt and pepper
Flour for dusting fish fillets
Oil for frying
Lemon wedges
Parsley for garnish

Batter
150g (1¼ cups) all purpose flour
230ml (1 cup) beer
10ml (2 tsp) olive oil
Salt
2 eggs, separated

METHOD

1. Arrange the fish fillets in a glass dish and sprinkle them with lemon juice, salt, and pepper.
2. Leave to stand for 30 minutes.
3. Prepare the batter by whisking all the ingredients except the egg whites to a smooth, liquid consistency.
4. Beat the egg whites until they are stiff and fold them into the batter.
5. Dust the fillets with flour and dip them in the batter.
6. Heat the oil in a deep frying pan and fry the fillets for 8-12 minutes or until they are golden brown.
7. Drain them on a paper towel and serve hot, garnished with lemon wedges and parsley.

Nice served with tartare sauce.

MEAT & POULTRY

Fillet of Beef Napoleon En Croute

Fillet of Beef Napoleon En Croute

INGREDIENTS
Serves 4

Beef Napoleon
4 fillet steaks 150g-210g
(¼-½ lb)
30ml (2 Tbsp) cooking oil
Salt and pepper
1 shallot
60g (¼ cup) butter
240g (½ lb) mushrooms,
chopped
60g (2 oz) morels or
other mushrooms
30ml (2 Tbsp) Calvados
(apple brandy)
360g (1½ lb) puff pastry

For the Garnish and Sauce
110g (¼ lb) carrots, shaped
110g (¼ lb) turnips, shaped
12 morels or mushrooms
60ml (¼ cup) Calvados
60ml (¼ cup) port
5ml (1 tsp) tomato paste
150ml (⅔ cup) brown sauce
60ml (¼ cup) stock bouillon
60g (¼ cup) butter
Cayenne pepper
Salt
1 shallot

METHOD

1. Sear fillet steaks in oil. Season and allow to cool.
2. Cook finely chopped shallot in a little butter without allowing it to colour. Add the chopped mushrooms and morels.
3. Add Calvados and cook until all the liquid has evaporated. Cool mixture.
4. Roll out puff pastry ¼-½ cm (⅛-¼ inch) thick; keep as square as possible. Cut into quarters.
5. Place equal amounts of the cold mushroom mixture on the pastry, then place a fillet steak on the mushroom mixture. Wrap up each fillet in pastry.
6. Turn over onto a baking sheet, presentation side up.
7. Brush with milk or beaten egg; allow to relax in the refrigerator for 30-50 minutes.
8. Bake in an oven, 240°C (450°F), or Gas mark 9, for 20-30 minutes.

Fillet of Beef Napoleon En Croute

CONTINUED

9. Cook the vegetables for the garnish in salted water, keeping the carrots and turnips slightly underdone. Drain. Add morels or mushrooms and butter to the drained vegetables. Cook gently for 1-2 minutes. Season and reserve.
10. Shallow fry the finely chopped shallot in thick bottomed pan in a small amount of butter.
11. When golden brown, add Calvados, port, and tomato paste, and reduce by half.
12. Add sauce and stock, and continue reducing until the desired consistency of sauce is obtained (not too thick).
13. Shake or whisk in small pieces of butter.
14. Do not let sauce boil.
15. To serve, place fillets on a dish or plate, garnish with the vegetables, and serve the sauce separately.

Chicken in Creamed Pear Sauce

INGREDIENTS
Serves 4

4 chicken breasts, 150g (⅓ lb) each, boneless
4 pears
180ml (¾ cup) double cream (whipping cream)
1 endive
1 carrot, roughly chopped
1 stick celery, roughly chopped
Salt and pepper
300ml (1½ cups) chicken stock (bouillon), divided
75g (½ cup) wild rice
75g (½ cup) Carolina rice
½ bunch watercress
30ml (2 Tbsp) cooking oil
1 onion
45g (3 Tbsp) butter

METHOD

1. Trim breasts of all skin.
2. Peel and core the pears and poach in 100ml (½ cup) chicken stock. (Save pear peelings.)
3. Remove and purée half the pears and retain the rest.
4. Add carrot, celery, and pear peelings to the stock used for poaching and cook to obtain a good stock.
5. Cook the chopped onion in oil until transparent.
6. Add the two types of rice and 200ml (1 cup) of chicken stock.
7. Season and cover with a buttered greaseproof paper and lid.
8. Cook for 20 minutes at 230°C (450°F), Gas mark 7. When cooked, turn out onto a dish. Add the butter, and mix in.
9. Cover and keep hot.
10. While the rice is cooking, steam the chicken breasts over the boiling chicken stock (which includes the vegetables, pear skin, etc.) for 15-20 minutes.

Chicken in Creamed Pear Sauce

CONTINUED

11. The sauce is made by reducing the cream to a coating consistency and then adding the pear purée.
12. Retain some of the endive leaves to decorate.
13. Shred the remainder and add to the sauce.
14. Re-boil and cook for 1-2 minutes. Check seasoning.
15. To serve, place a layer of rice on a serving dish. Cut each breast 4-5 times on the slant and arrange on the rice.
16. Coat with sauce and garnish with the hot poached pear, watercress, and endive leaves.

Blackcurrant Chicken

INGREDIENTS

Serves 4

4 chicken breasts
115ml (½ cup) red wine
120g (½ cup) blackcurrant jelly or redcurrant jelly
2-3 bay leaves
Salt and pepper

METHOD

1. Place chicken breasts in ovenproof dish, pour on red wine, season with salt and pepper.
2. Add 2-3 bay leaves. Add blackcurrant or redcurrant jelly. Cover the dish with a lid.
3. Cook for 40 minutes at 200°C (400°F), Gas mark 6, or until thoroughly cooked.
4. Serve with new potatoes and broccoli.

David's Duckling

INGREDIENTS
Serves 4

1.8kg (4 lb) duckling
Salt and pepper
4 small onions stuck with cloves
25g (2 Tbsp) butter or oil
30ml (2 Tbsp) brandy or rum
10ml (2 tsp) cornflour (cornstarch)
150ml (2/3 cup) stock
60ml (1/4 cup) Cumberland sauce (recipe on p. 163)

METHOD

1. Wipe the bird and sprinkle inside and out with salt and pepper. Put the onions stuck with cloves inside the body. Rub with butter or oil and roast at 200°C (400°F), or Gas mark 6, for 1 hour 40 minutes, basting from time to time.
2. When cooked, pour off excess fat. Warm the brandy, pour it over and set alight.
3. Put duck on to a warmed serving dish.
4. Stir 1 Tbsp water into the cornflour and then stir into the pan juices. Add the stock, and then add the Cumberland sauce. Stir and simmer for about 5 minutes.
5. Pour a little sauce over the duck and serve the rest in a sauceboat.

Braised Duck

INGREDIENTS

Serves 4

> 4 duck breasts, 200g-225g (½ lb)
> 275ml (1¼ cup) sherry
> 55ml (¼ cup) soy sauce
> 115g (½ cup) Demerara sugar (natural brown sugar)
> 5ml (1 tsp) ground ginger
> 5ml (1 tsp) cornflour (cornstarch)

METHOD

1. Score the duck in parallel lines across the skin.
2. Seal (sear) the duck in a hot, dry pan, skin side down, until golden in colour.
3. Turn and seal (sear) flesh side for 2 minutes.
4. Meanwhile mix together sherry, soy sauce, sugar, and ginger.
5. Lay the duck breasts skin side up in an ovenproof dish and cover with the liquor and then cover with a tight fitting lid.
6. Braise in the oven for 1½ hours, at 200°C (400°F), Gas mark 6.
7. Remove the duck from the liquor and keep warm.
8. Pour the liquor into a pan and skim off any excess duck fat.
9. Bring to the boil and thicken with cornflour to a coat consistency. (Mix the cornflour with 2 Tbsp water and then stir into the sauce until thickened.)

Serve the breasts on top of parsnip mash with the sauce poured over and stir fried pak choi (bok choi) and spring onions to accompany.

This recipe is the creation of our Head Chef, Steve Ramli-Davies.

Apple and Pork Loaf

INGREDIENTS

Serves 4-6

> 450g (1 lb) lean raw pork, minced
> 110g (¾ cup) rolled oats
> 350g (¾ lb) cooked apples, chopped and sieved
> 1 large egg
> 5ml (1 tsp) mixed herbs
> 2ml (½ tsp) Tabasco sauce
> Tomato sauce

METHOD

1. In a basin mix all ingredients together until evenly blended.
2. Press these ingredients well down into a 1½ lb greased loaf tin or similar tin.
3. Cover and bake at 180°C (350°F), or Gas mark 4, for about 1¼ hours.
4. When cooked, turn out on to a serving dish and serve with hot tomato sauce.

Somerset Casserole

INGREDIENTS
Serves 4-6

225g (½ lb) dried prunes
Orange juice
1kg (2.2 lb) diced pork
1 large onion, chopped
150ml (⅔ cup) cider
Bay leaf
Pepper
300ml (1⅓ cups) good chicken stock
15ml (3 Tbsp) redcurrant jelly
Freshly ground black pepper
25g (3 Tbsp) cornflour (cornstarch)
30ml (2 Tbsp) malt vinegar
Fresh parsley, chopped

METHOD

1. In one bowl combine the prunes and enough orange juice to cover them.
2. In another bowl combine pork, onion, cider, and bay leaf.
3. Leave both overnight in the fridge.
4. Place the pork and its marinade in a saucepan; add the chicken stock and redcurrant jelly.
5. Season with pepper and bring to the boil.
6. Drain the prunes (saving the liquid) and add to casserole, cover and cook for 1½ hours at 160°C (325°F), Gas mark 3, or until the pork is tender.
7. Pour the reserved liquid into another pan, blend the cornflour with the vinegar and stir this into the liquid.
8. Bring to the boil to thicken and simmer for 3 minutes, stirring all the time.
9. Pour the sauce over the pork, sprinkle with chopped parsley and serve.

Bacon and Apple Hotpot

INGREDIENTS
Serves 4-6

1.4kg (3 lb) boiling bacon (see note below)
450g (1 lb) peeled, cored, and sliced apples
1 large sliced onion
Pinch of sage and thyme
30ml (2 Tbsp) black treacle (molasses)
1 medium cabbage heart, quartered
Salt and pepper to taste.

METHOD

1. Trim the bacon and cut into large cubes. Soak for at least four hours in cold water.
2. Drain and put into a saucepan with the apples, onion, herbs, treacle, and pepper and cover with cold water. Bring to the boil and simmer gently for about 1 hour, or until the bacon is quite tender.
3. Add the cabbage, bring back to the boil, and then simmer again until the cabbage is cooked. Taste for seasoning and serve with boiled potatoes, which can be added with the cabbage, but see that they are all the same size so that cooking is even.

Note: Boiling bacon is unlike American-style bacon; it is cut from the pork shoulder or back and is much leaner than our bacon. In flavor, it resembles ham, and is sold in chunks, not strips.

Spring Lamb Roast

INGREDIENTS
Serves 4-6

1 shoulder of lamb, boned

Filling
25g (2 Tbsp) butter
1 medium onion, finely chopped
1 small lemon
20g (2 Tbsp) fresh chopped mint
225g (2 cups) fresh breadcrumbs
1 egg, beaten
Salt and pepper

Sauce
150ml (2/3 cup) vinegar
20g (2 Tbsp) fresh chopped mint
10ml (2 tsp) caster sugar (granulated sugar)
15ml (1 Tbsp) honey
15ml (1 Tbsp) soy sauce
5ml (1 tsp) cornflour (cornstarch)
275ml (1¼ cup) water

METHOD

Filling
1. Melt butter in a pan. Add onion and lightly fry for 5 minutes.
2. Grate rind from lemon, discard pith and cut flesh into ¼ inch cubes. Mix all filling ingredients well.
3. Place filling in cavity left by bone. Press into shape and secure with string.
4. Sprinkle with salt and pepper and put in a roasting tin.
5. Roast at 200°C (400°F) or Gas mark 6 for 1½ hours, or until meat is cooked.

Sauce
6. Place all ingredients, except for the cornflour and water, in a saucepan and bring to the boil.
7. Blend cornflour with the water, stir into the sauce, bring to the boil, stirring all the time, and cook for 1 minute.
8. To serve, put meat on a serving dish, remove string and garnish with cooked vegetables.
9. Serve sauce separately.

Lancashire Hotpot

INGREDIENTS
Serves 4-6

600g (1¼ lb) lean stewing lamb
2 large onions, sliced
30ml (2 Tbsp) cooking oil
480g (½ lb) potatoes, peeled and sliced
900ml (4 cups) stock (bouillon)
Salt and pepper
3 sprigs parsley

METHOD

1. Trim lamb of excess fat and skin.
2. Fry in the oil until golden brown, drain and reserve.
3. Add the sliced onions to the pan. Fry to a golden brown.
4. In an oven to table casserole dish, place layers of sliced potatoes, sliced onion, and meat until the meat and onions are used up. Finish off the top with overlapping slices of potato.
5. Add seasoning and stock.
6. Cook in a moderate oven, 180°C (350°F), Gas mark 4, for 1½-2 hours.
7. When cooked, the top will be rich brown.
8. Serve sprinkled with chopped parsley.

Moussaka

INGREDIENTS
Serves 4

Fresh Tomato Sauce
37ml (½ cup) olive oil
125g (½ cup) onion,
    finely chopped
1 stalk celery,
    finely chopped
1 can Italian tomatoes,
    chopped
30ml (2 Tbsp) tomato paste
1 bay leaf
6 basil leaves, or
    5ml (1 tsp) dried
Salt and freshly
    ground pepper

Moussaka
2 egg yolks, beaten
230ml (1 cup) milk
Salt and freshly
    ground pepper
1 small onion, sliced
115ml (½ cup) olive oil
    (divided)
4 eggplants, sliced
500g (½ lb) cooked
    minced lamb
115ml (½ cup) beef stock
115ml (½ cup) fresh
    tomato sauce

METHOD

Tomato sauce
1. Heat the oil in a heavy-based pan and cook the onion and celery.
2. When the onion is golden, add the tomatoes, tomato paste, bay leaf, basil, salt, and pepper.
3. Bring to the boil. Reduce the heat and simmer, uncovered, stirring occasionally, for 45 minutes or until thickened.
4. This sauce goes with spaghetti and other pastas.

Moussaka
1. Combine the egg yolks, milk, salt, and pepper, and cook over a low heat, stirring constantly, until it is like a thick custard.
2. Set aside to cool.
3. Cook the onion in 1 Tbsp of the oil until golden brown.
4. Lightly fry the eggplant slices in the remaining oil.

Moussaka

CONTINUED

5. Oil the bottom and sides of a casserole dish 5cm (2 inch) deep.
6. Cover the bottom with a layer of eggplant and place some minced lamb and fried onions on top.
7. Repeat the layers until the ingredients are all used.
8. Pour the beef or lamb stock and tomato sauce on top and cover with the custard.
9. Bake the dish in an oven preheated to 180°C (350°F), or Gas mark 4, for at least 1 hour, or until the top has formed a golden brown crust.
10. Serve hot or cold with a crisp salad.

Hamburg Steak

A fried or baked cake of freshly minced and seasoned steak, very popular in the United States. Popularity is also increasing in Great Britain, with many hamburger houses and restaurants now open. Hamburgers are usually served inside a soft bap (large soft roll).

INGREDIENTS
Serves 4-6

.5kg (1 lb) lean beef, chuck, shoulder, or rump steak
½ onion, skinned and grated, optional
Salt and pepper
Oil for shallow frying

METHOD

1. Choose lean meat and have it finely minced by the butcher.
2. Mix well with onion (if used) and a generous amount of salt and pepper.
3. Shape lightly into 6-8 round, flat cakes.
4. To cook, brush sparingly with oil and grill for 4-6 minutes turning once, or fry in a little oil in the frying pan, turning them once and allowing the same amount of time.

Hamburgers can be served rare or well done, according to personal preference, hence the variation in cooking time.

Traditionally, hamburgers contain no other ingredients, but they can be varied by adding any of the following when mixing the hamburgers: 50g-100g (½ cup-1 cup) grated cheese, 1 Tbsp mixed sweet pickle, 1 tsp dried mixed herbs, 1 Tbsp chopped parsley, 50g (1 cup) chopped mushrooms.

Goulash

A rich meat stew flavoured with paprika, Hungarian in origin but found in several European countries. Soured cream can be stirred in or served separately.

INGREDIENTS
Serves 4-6

.75kg (1½ lb) stewing steak, cut into 1cm (½ inch) cubes
45g (6 Tbsp) seasoned flour
2 medium sized onions, skinned and chopped
1 green pepper, seeded and chopped
30ml (2 Tbsp) oil
20g (2 Tbsp) paprika
45ml (3 Tbsp) tomato paste
5ml (1 tsp) nutmeg
Salt and pepper
50g (6 Tbsp) flour
300ml (1¼ cups) stock
2 large tomatoes, skinned and quartered
Bouquet garni (see p 170)
150ml (⅔ cup) beer

METHOD

1. Coat the meat with seasoned flour.
2. Fry the onions and pepper lightly in oil for about 3 to 4 minutes.
3. Add the meat and fry lightly on all sides until golden brown, about 5 minutes.
4. Add the paprika and fry for about a minute longer.
5. Stir in the tomato paste, nutmeg, seasoning, and flour and cook for a further 2 to 3 minutes.
6. Add the stock, tomatoes, and bouquet garni. Put into a casserole and cook in a moderate oven, 160°C (325°F), Gas mark 3, for 1½ to 2 hours.
7. Add the beer. Cook for a few minutes longer and remove the bouquet garni.
8. Serve with sauerkraut or green salad and sour cream.

Meatballs – Greek and American

INGREDIENTS
Serves 4

Meatballs
1 large onion, very finely chopped
450g (1 lb) finely minced lean beef or lamb
110g (1 cup) fresh breadcrumbs
1 egg beaten
28g (2 Tbsp) chopped fresh parsley
14g (1 Tbsp) chopped fresh oregano
Salt and freshly ground black pepper to taste
55g (½ cup) plain flour
30ml (2 Tbsp) vegetable oil

METHOD
Meatballs
1. Mix thoroughly together in a large bowl the onion, meat, breadcrumbs, egg, parsley, oregano, salt, and pepper.
2. Form the mixture into balls, taking a teaspoonful at a time and rolling it in the palms of your hands, then in the flour.
3. Heat the oil in a heavy frying pan. Add the meatballs and fry them, a few at a time, for about 4 minutes, turning once.
4. Transfer the meatballs to a warm dish and keep them warm in a low oven.

Meatballs – Greek and American

CONTINUED

Tomato Sauce
45ml (3 Tbsp) olive oil
1 small onion, finely chopped
1 clove garlic, finely chopped
900g (2 lb) tomatoes,
 peeled and chopped
14g (1 Tbsp) fresh basil,
 finely chopped
2 bay leaves
Salt
Freshly ground black pepper

Greek Sauce
150ml (⅔ cup) natural
 yogurt
1 Tbsp cornflour
 (cornstarch)
⅔ cup water
Pan juices

METHOD

Fresh American Tomato Sauce
1. To peel the tomatoes, drop them into boiling water for about 30 seconds, then drain immediately. The skins will slip off easily.
2. Heat the oil in a saucepan on a medium heat. Add the onion and garlic and cook until the onion is soft and just beginning to brown.
3. Add the tomatoes, salt, and pepper and simmer gently, uncovered, for about 30 minutes.
4. Add the basil and bay leaves and cook the sauce for 10 minutes more. Remove the bay leaves and serve with the meatballs.

Piquant Greek Sauce
1. Whisk together natural yogurt with water and cornflour.
2. Add this mixture to the pan juices left after frying the meatballs and heat together, stirring constantly, until the sauce thickens.
3. Adjust the seasoning to taste and return the meatballs to the pan to coat them with sauce.

Spaghetti alla Bolognese

INGREDIENTS

Serves 4

1 medium onion
1 stalk celery
1 carrot
125g (¼ lb) bacon
50g (4 Tbsp) butter
250g (½ lb) minced lean beef
Salt and pepper
Pinch of nutmeg
4 fresh oregano leaves, chopped or 2ml (½ tsp), dried
115ml (½ cup) dry white wine
230ml (1 cup) good beef stock
50g (3 Tbsp) tomato paste
375g (¾ lb) spaghetti
115ml (½ cup) heavy cream
Parmesan cheese

METHOD

1. Chop the onion, celery, carrot, and bacon very fine, then cook with butter in a heavy-based pan until the onion is soft and translucent.
2. Add the beef and cook until the beef changes colour.
3. Season well with salt, black pepper, nutmeg, and oregano. Increase the heat before pouring in the wine.
4. Bring to the boil, stirring constantly, and continue cooking until the wine has almost entirely evaporated.
5. Add the stock and tomato paste and simmer for 35-40 minutes over a low heat.
6. Stir frequently. When the sauce has been simmering for some 25-30 minutes, cook the spaghetti in a large pot of boiling, salted water until al dente. Drain.
7. Add the cream to the sauce.
8. Mix the spaghetti and sauce well. Serve sprinkled with Parmesan cheese.

Fillet Steak in Green Pepper Sauce

The Royal Family love good food. Here is one of their recipes.

INGREDIENTS
Serves 4

4 x 180g (¼ lb) fillet steaks, middle cut and trimmed
60g (¼ cup) butter
15g (1 Tbsp) cooking oil
Salt and pepper
1 green pimento (green bell pepper)
1 small onion
3 Tbsp brandy
150ml (⅔ cup) brown sauce (method below)
120ml (½ cup) single cream (half and half)
48 green peppercorns

METHOD
1. Fry the steaks in oil and butter in a thick bottomed pan.
2. Season with salt and freshly ground pepper. Cook until done as required.
3. Remove steaks, add pimento and onion cut into small dice, and cook for 2-3 minutes.
4. Drain off excess fat.
5. Flame the brandy to combine with the residue, and add the brown sauce.
6. Bring to the boil, add cream, remove from heat, and correct seasoning.
7. Place steaks onto a serving dish.
8. Press twelve green peppercorns into each steak and coat with sauce.

Brown Sauce
1. Melt 1 Tbsp butter; stir in 1½ Tbsp flour. Stir and cook until browned. Add 1 cup stock (bouillon); stir until thickened and smooth.

Carbonade of Beef

INGREDIENTS
Serves 6-8

1.35kg (3 lb) braising steak (chuck)
Salt and freshly ground black pepper
30g (2 Tbsp) olive oil
30g (2 Tbsp) butter
680g (1½ lbs) onions, peeled and sliced
15g (2 Tbsp) flour
600ml (2½ cups) brown ale

METHOD

1. Cut the steak into large cubes and season generously with salt and pepper.
2. Heat the oil in a heavy flameproof casserole. Add the meat and brown it quickly on all sides.
3. Lift out the beef and add butter to the casserole.
4. Reduce the heat. Add the onions and brown them evenly without allowing them to burn.
5. Sprinkle the onions with the flour and mix well.
6. Return the meat to the casserole and add the beer.
7. Bring to the boil on top of the stove.
8. Cover the casserole tightly and cook in preheated slow oven, 150°C (300°F), Gas mark 2, for three hours, or until the meat is very tender.
9. Adjust the seasoning and serve the carbonade piping hot with plenty of fluffy mashed potato or with flat ribbons of pasta.
10. The dish tastes even better if it is cooled and reheated, and cooling makes it easier to remove any surplus fat from the gravy. It freezes well too.

Traditional Cornish Pasties

INGREDIENTS
Serves 4

Short Crust Pastry
100g (½ cup) margarine
100g (½ cup) lard (may substitute shortening)
350g (2¾ cups) plain flour
45ml (3 Tbsp) water
Pinch of salt

Filling
350g (¾ lb) chuck steak
100g (¼ lb) raw potato, peeled and diced
1 onion, chopped
40g (2 oz) swede (rutabaga), peeled and diced
Salt and pepper

METHOD

1. Sift flour and salt.
2. Rub in the margarine and lard.
3. Make a bay and add water; work to a paste.
4. Allow to stand in a cool place for 30 minutes.
5. Cut the steak into small pieces, add the potato, onion, and swede, and season well.
6. Divide the pastry into four and roll each piece into a round 20cm (8 inch) in diameter.
7. Divide the meat mixture between the pastry rounds.
8. Dampen the edge, draw the edges of the pastry rounds together to form a seam across the top, and flute the edges with your fingers.
9. Place on a baking sheet and bake in a hot oven, 220°C (425°F), Gas mark 7, for 15 minutes to brown the pastry, then reduce the oven to moderate, 160°C (320°F), Gas mark 3, and cook for a further hour.
10. Serve hot or cold.

Honey-baked Virginia Ham

INGREDIENTS
Serves 10+

1 large whole ham
10 coriander seeds
6 peppercorns
3 bay leaves
Water
Honey
Cloves

METHOD

1. Soak ham for 24 hours in cold water.
2. Drain, place in a suitable pan. Cover with fresh water plus coriander seeds, peppercorns, and bay leaves.
3. Bring to the boil, simmer for 25 minutes per .5kg (1 lb) plus an extra 25 minutes.
4. Allow to cool in the cooking liquid.
5. Remove the rind and trim off excess fat.
6. Stud with cloves at about 4cm (2 inch) intervals all over the surface. Baste with honey.
7. Place the ham on a suitable tray in a very hot oven, 240°C (475°F), Gas mark 9. Baste with honey from time to time.
8. Allow to colour a light brown.
9. Remove from oven. Allow to cool.

A piece of cooked ham may be treated with cloves and honey in the same manner. Do not add salt to water when cooking ham, as there is usually more than sufficient salt in the ham.

Hot Game Pie

INGREDIENTS

Serves 4-6

1kg (2.2 lb) venison, wild duck, or pheasant
30g (2 Tbsp) butter or cooking oil
600ml (2½ cups) stock (bouillon)
1 sprig thyme
1 bay leaf
300ml (1⅓ cups) red wine
1 small onion
15g (1 Tbsp) butter
Salt and pepper
360g (1¾ lb) puff pastry
1 beaten egg

METHOD

1. Remove the flesh from the bones and skin, and cut into bite size pieces. Fry in butter to give a rich colour, then drain.
2. Prepare a game sauce using the bones cooked in the stock to give a game flavour.
3. Season with thyme and bay leaf.
4. Strain this over the game and add the red wine, onion (chopped and cooked without colouring in a little butter), salt, and pepper.
5. Simmer for one hour approximately on a low heat until tender.
6. Pour into pie dish and allow to cool.
7. Cover the top with puff pastry ¼cm (¹⁄₁₀ inch) thick and allow to relax for half an hour.
8. Brush with beaten egg and bake in a hot oven, 200°C (400°F), or Gas mark 6, for 20 minutes.

EGGS

Omelette

OMELETTES

With care, anyone can master the art of omelette making. Delicate handling is needed, but a little practice makes perfect – do not be discouraged if your first two or three omelettes are not successful.

Two points about omelettes that make them particularly convenient are the short time they take to make and the way they use up odds and ends such as cooked meat, fish, or vegetables, either in the omelette itself as a filling or as an accompaniment.

Have everything ready before beginning to make an omelette, including the hot plate on which to serve it. An omelette must never wait but rather be waited for.

Omelette pan: Special little omelette pans are obtainable and should be kept for omelettes only. However, if you do not own such a pan, a thick-based frying pan can equally well be used. Whether of cast iron, copper, or aluminium, the pan should be thick so that it will hold sufficient heat to cook the egg mixture as soon as it is put in. Thus the omelette can be in and out of the pan in about 2 minutes.

One of the essentials of success: slow cooking and over-cooking both make an omelette tough.

A 15cm (6 inch) to 18cm (7 inch) pan takes a 2-3 egg omelette.

To season an omelette pan, put 15ml spoon (1 Tbsp) salt in the pan, heat it slowly, then rub well in with a piece of kitchen paper. Tip away the salt and wipe the pan with kitchen paper.

To clean the omelette pan after use, do not wash it but rub it over with a clean cloth.

Non-stick pans are ideal for omelettes and do not need seasoning.

A few minutes before you want to cook an omelette, place the pan on a very gentle heat to ensure that it is heated evenly right to the edges. A fierce heat would cause the pan to heat unevenly. When the pan is ready for the mixture it will feel comfortably hot if you hold the back of your hand about 2.5cm (1 inch) away from the surface.

Fat for greasing omelette pans: Butter gives the best flavour, but bacon fat is very good too.

TYPES OF OMELETTES

Basically, there are only two different kinds, the plain and the soufflé omelette, in which the egg whites are whisked separately and folded into the yolk mixture, giving it a fluffy texture.

Plain omelettes are almost invariably savoury and soufflé omelettes are most commonly served as a sweet. There are, of course, many different omelette variations achieved by the different ingredients added to the eggs or used in the filling.

Plain Omelette

INGREDIENTS

Serves 1

2 eggs
Salt and freshly ground black pepper

METHOD

1. Allow two eggs per person. Whisk them just enough to break down the eggs; don't make them frothy as overbeating spoils the texture of the finished omelette.
2. Season with salt and pepper and add 15ml spoon (1 Tbsp) water.
3. Place the pan over a gentle heat and when it is hot add a knob (2 Tbsp, more or less) of butter to grease it lightly.
4. Pour the beaten eggs into the hot butter.
5. Stir gently with the back of the prongs of a fork, drawing the mixture from the side to the centre as it sets and letting the liquid egg from the centre run to the sides.
6. When the egg has set, stop stirring and cook for another minute until it is golden underneath and still creamy on top.
7. Tilt the pan away from you slightly, and use a palette knife to fold over a third of the omelette into the centre, then fold over the opposite third of the omelette out onto the warmed plate, with the folded sides underneath, and serve at once.
8. Do not overcook or the omelette will be tough.

Omelette Fillings

FILLING OPTIONS (PER OMELETTE)

Herbs
Add 2 Tbsp finely chopped, fresh herbs to the beaten egg mixture before cooking. Parsley, chives, chervil, and tarragon are all suitable.

Cheese
Grate 40g (1½ oz) cheese and mix 3 Tbsp of it with the egg before cooking. Sprinkle the rest over the omelette after it is folded.

Tomato
Peel and chop 1-2 tomatoes and fry in a little butter in a saucepan for five minutes, until soft and pulpy. Put in the centre of the omelette before folding.

Mushroom
Wash and slice 50g (2 oz) mushrooms and cook in butter in a saucepan until soft. Put in the centre of the omelette before folding.

Bacon
Rind and scissor snip two rashers (slices) of bacon and fry in a pan until crisp. Put in the centre of the omelette before folding.

Ham
Chop 50g (2 oz) of cooked ham. Add 1 tsp chopped parsley to the beaten egg before cooking. Put ham in the centre of the omelette before folding.

Fish
Flake some cooked fish and heat gently in a little cream. Put in the centre of the omelette before folding.

Omelette Arnold Bennett

INGREDIENTS

Serves 1-2

100g (¼ lb) smoked haddock, poached
50g (¼ cup) butter, divided
150ml (⅔ cup) double cream (whipping cream), divided
3 eggs, separated
30g (¼ cup) grated Parmesan cheese
Salt and freshly ground black pepper

METHOD

1. Flake the cooked fish, removing any skin and bones.
2. Place the fish in a saucepan with half the butter and 2 Tbsps cream.
3. Toss over a high heat until the butter melts, then leave it to cool.
4. Beat the eggs with 1 Tbsp of cream, 1 Tbsp Parmesan cheese, and seasonings. Stir in the fish mixture. Stiffly whisk the egg whites and fold into the mixture.
5. Melt the remaining butter in an omelette pan and cook the omelette in the usual way, but do not fold over.
6. Slide omelette onto a heatproof plate, top with the remaining cheese and cream blended together, then quickly bubble under a pre-heated grill (broiler).

Spanish Omelette

INGREDIENTS

Serves 3-4

45ml (3 Tbsp) olive oil
2 large potatoes, peeled and cut into 1cm (½ inch) cubes
2 large onions, skinned and chopped
Salt and freshly ground black pepper
6 eggs, lightly beaten

METHOD

1. In a medium sized frying pan, gently heat the olive oil.
2. Add potatoes and onions and season with salt and pepper. Cook for 10-15 minutes, stirring occasionally, until golden brown.
3. Drain off the excess oil and gently stir in the eggs.
4. Cook for 5 minutes, shaking the pan occasionally to prevent sticking.
5. If you wish, place under a hot grill (broiler) to brown the top.
6. Turn onto a warmed serving plate.

Yorkshire Pudding

INGREDIENTS

Serves 4-6

>110g (1 cup) plain flour
>5ml (1 tsp) salt
>2 eggs
>150ml (⅔ cup) milk or milk and water
>55ml (¼ cup) oil

METHOD

1. Put flour and salt into a mixing bowl.
2. Make a well in the centre and break in the eggs.
3. Whisk gradually to mix in the flour. When the eggs are almost mixed, add the milk and make into a smooth batter.
4. Leave batter to stand for 15 minutes to soften.
5. Heat the oil in 12 Yorkshire pudding tins. When the oil is very hot, pour in the batter.
6. Bake at the top of the oven at 220°C (425°F) or Gas mark 7, for 20-25 minutes or until well risen and crispy, golden brown.

You may use custard cups or muffin tins.

SAVOURIES

Chicken and Leek Pie

Chicken and Leek Pie

INGREDIENTS
Serves 4-6

Pastry
225g (2 cups) plain flour
5ml (1 tsp) salt
185g (14 Tbsp) butter
29ml (5 Tbsp) water

Filling
1.5kg (3.3 lb) chicken thighs
845ml (3 cups) good chicken stock
3-4 leeks, split and sliced
25g (2 Tbsp) butter
25g (¼ cup) flour
15ml (1 Tbsp) cream
Salt and pepper
Egg glaze

METHOD

Pastry
1. Sift the flour and salt into a bowl.
2. Add the butter and rub in until the mixture resembles fine breadcrumbs.
3. Add water, mixing lightly until the dough becomes smooth. Roll into a ball and rest for 20 minutes or until required.

Filling
1. Cook the chicken in the stock until tender.
2. Lift the cooked chicken from the stock and set aside to cool, reserving the cooking liquid.
3. Blanch the leeks for 1 minute in some of the boiling stock, strain and set aside.
4. Remove and discard the skin and bones of the chicken. Cut the chicken meat into chunky pieces.
5. Melt the butter. Stir in the flour and cook for 1-2 minutes without browning.

Chicken and Leek Pie

CONTINUED

6. Gradually add some of the reserved stock, stirring between each addition until the sauce is smooth and thickened.
7. Simmer for 2-3 minutes and remove from the heat.
8. Add the cream and season well with salt and pepper.
9. Roll out half the pastry to line a 23-25cm (9-10 inch) pie plate. Spread the chicken and leeks over the pastry.
10. Add some of the sauce to the chicken. Brush the pastry edge lightly with water.
11. Roll out the remaining pastry. Cover the pie, trim and seal the edges firmly. Cut a small slit in the top of the pastry and brush lightly with the egg glaze.
12. Bake in the centre of an oven preheated to 200°C (400°F), Gas mark 6, for 30 minutes or until the pastry is golden brown.

Serve hot or cold.

Basic Pizza

INGREDIENTS FOR PIZZA DOUGH
Makes dough for 2 medium-large pizzas

> 250ml (1 cup) milk
> 2ml (½ tsp) sugar (if using fresh or granular dried yeast)
> 15g (1 Tbsp) fresh yeast or 5ml (1 tsp) granular dried yeast,
>   or 5ml (1 tsp) easy blend dried yeast
> 450g (3½ cups) strong plain white (bread) flour
> 5ml (1 tsp) salt
> 1 large egg
> 90ml (6 Tbsp) olive oil

METHODS

Using fresh yeast or granular dried yeast
1. Heat the milk to lukewarm 43°C (110°F) and mix about one third of it with the sugar and yeast in a small bowl.
2. Leave mixture to stand until it can be stirred easily into a cream.
3. Sift the flour and salt into a large bowl.
4. Mix the remaining warm milk with the egg and oil and stir lightly together.
5. Make a well in the centre of the flour and pour in the yeast and egg mixtures all at once.
6. Use a fork to mix the ingredients to a dough.

Using easy blend dried yeast
1. Sift together into a large bowl the flour, yeast, and salt.
2. Add the egg mixture to the flour all at once and mix to form a dough.

Continue
1. Turn the dough, which will be very sticky at this stage, onto a well-floured surface and knead it for about 5 minutes, or until the dough is springy and elastic.
2. Form into a ball and put in a plastic bag, or cover with plastic food wrap, and leave in a warm place for one to three hours. Too high a temperature will kill the yeast, so do not be tempted to hurry the rising process.

Basic Pizza

CONTINUED

3. The dough will rise perfectly well in its own time in a cool temperature, which means that it can be left overnight to rise.
4. Punch the risen dough down to knock the air out of it and knead briefly on a floured surface before separating it into two balls and rolling out with a floured rolling pin.
5. Pizza dough should generally be rolled fairly thinly– 7mm (¼ inch) thick is generally quite thick enough.
6. To store risen dough in the refrigerator, punch it down and re-form it into one or two balls. Return to the bowl, cover and refrigerate for up to four days. The warmth of the dough may cause it to rise a little before it cools down, and when needed it can be used straight from the refrigerator.

INGREDIENTS FOR PIZZA SAUCE

Makes sauce for 2 medium-large pizzas

> 900g (2 lb) onions, sliced and cut thin into rings
> 2 cloves garlic, finely chopped
> 900g (2 lb) tin plum tomatoes with their juice
> 5ml (1 tsp) dried marjoram or oregano
> Salt and ground black pepper

METHOD

1. Heat the oil in a large pan and add the onions.
2. Cook slowly, uncovered, on a gentle heat for about 20 minutes, or until they are soft but not coloured.
3. Add garlic and cook for a few minutes more before adding the tomatoes and the juice. Add marjoram or oregano, and salt and pepper to taste.

Continued

Basic Pizza

CONTINUED

4. Cook slowly, uncovered, on a low heat for about 40 minutes, or until the sauce starts to thicken and much of the juice has evaporated.
5. Stir the sauce from time to time to prevent it from sticking, and break up the tomatoes against the side of the pan with a wooden spoon.
6. Leave to cool. Use as required.

INGREDIENTS FOR COOKING PIZZA

As Desired

> *Beef, browned or cooked*
> *Sausage, cooked*
> *Ham, cooked*
> *Pepperoni*
> *Other cooked meats or fishes*
> *Peppers*
> *Mushrooms*
> *Onions*
> *Tomatoes*
> *Spinach*
> *Other vegetables or ingredients*
> *Mozzarella (or other cheeses), shredded*

METHOD

1. Pre-heat oven to 180°C (350°F), Gas mark 4.
2. Roll balls of dough flat into thin circles—7mm (¼ inch) thick is generally quite thick enough.
3. Place rolled out dough on two lightly oiled pizza pans or baking sheets to keep the dough from sticking. The rolled out pizza dough should be pressed outward to cover most of the pizza pan. With your thumbs and index fingers pinch the outer edge all the way around like a pie crust.

Basic Pizza

CONTINUED

4. Using a palate knife or small brush, spread the sauce onto the rolled out dough in a circular pattern, spreading as thick or thin as desired.
5. Next, add any number of ingredients as desired, usually adding the cooked meats first, then vegetables and other non-cheese ingredients, all evenly placed around the pizza.
6. Add a generous amount of shredded cheese atop the other ingredients and spread evenly around the pizza.
7. Cook for 10-12 minutes or until the cheese is melted as desired.
8. Serve pizza with a lavish green salad, or lots of mixed salads, and inexpensive Italian wine. Add a very definite extra 'something' to the meal by passing round a bottle of hot, chilli-flavoured olive oil.

Canapé Ecossaise

INGREDIENTS

Serves 4-6

>4-6 *rounds of toast*
>30g *(2 Tbsp) butter*
>8 *eggs*
>15ml *(1 Tbsp) cream*
>8-12 *anchovy fillets*
>16-24 *capers*

METHOD

1. Butter toast, which has been cut with a round 6cm (3 inch) cutter.
2. Prepare scrambled egg mix. Add cream to broken eggs; mix well with fork or whisk.
3. Cook eggs to light and fluffy.
4. Heap the mixture evenly on toast.
5. Garnish with criss-cross of anchovy fillets.
6. Place a caper in each section.
7. Garnish with parsley.

Smoked Salmon Quiche

INGREDIENTS
Serves 4-6

Pastry
225g (1¼ cups) flour
150g (11 Tbsp) butter
Pinch of salt
30ml (2 Tbsp) water

Quiche
4 eggs
150ml (⅔ cup) double cream
    (whipping cream)
150ml (⅔ cup) milk
150ml (⅔ cup) well-flavoured
    fish stock
Salt and freshly ground pepper
Grated nutmeg
Shortcrust pastry
Thinly sliced smoked salmon
Butter

METHOD

Pastry
1. Sift flour and salt into a mixing bowl. Rub in butter with tips of fingers to a fine breadcrumbs mixture. Do this very gently and lightly, or the mixture will become heavy.
2. Add water, working into a dough with your fingers. Shape the moist dough into a round.
3. Place in a polythene (plastic) bag and leave in the fridge for one hour. The shortcrust pastry is now ready for lining the flan tin.
4. Line a flan tin with shortcrust pastry, prick the bottom and bake 'blind' in a hot oven, 230°C (450°F), Gas mark 8, for about 15 minutes, just long enough to set the pastry without browning it. Allow to cool.

Quiche
1. Whisk eggs together with cream, milk, and well-flavoured fish stock. When well mixed, season to taste with salt and pepper and nutmeg.
2. Fill pastry case with egg mixture. Cover with thin slices of smoked salmon and dot with butter.
3. Bake in a moderate oven, 160°C (320°F), Gas mark 3, for 30-40 minutes and serve immediately.

Quiche Lorraine

INGREDIENTS

Serves 4-6

Pastry
120g (1 cup) flour
30g (2 Tbsp) butter
30g (2 Tbsp) lard (may substitute shortening)
1 egg yolk
Pinch of salt
30ml (2 Tbsp) water

Filling
30g (2 oz) diced bacon
½ clove of garlic, chopped
1 egg
125ml (½ cup) milk
Seasoning
50g (½ cup) grated mature Cheddar cheese

METHOD

Pastry
1. Sift flour and salt into a bowl.
2. Rub in the fat (butter and lard).
3. Make a bay, add egg yolk and water. Work to a paste.
4. Line a 7 inch flan ring and allow to stand.

Filling
1. Heat the milk with the garlic.
2. Beat the eggs and seasoning.
3. Add the milk and mix well.
4. Fry the diced bacon and garnish the bottom of the pastry-lined flan ring.
5. Strain liquid over the top.
6. Sprinkle with cheese.
7. Cook in a moderate oven until firm.
8. Serve hot.

Baked Custard Pie

Baked egg custard pies must be kept refrigerated and must not be kept for more than 2-3 days.

INGREDIENTS
Serves 6-8

Pastry
225g (2 cups) plain flour
½ tsp salt
110g (½ cup) butter
50g (¼ cup) lard (may subsitute shortening)
29ml (2 Tbsp) water

Filling
4 large fresh eggs
150g (¾ cup) sugar
2ml (½ tsp) nutmeg
570ml (2½ cups) hot milk
5ml (1 tsp) vanilla essence
23-25 cm (9 inch) dish lined with shortcrust pastry

METHOD

Pastry
1. Sift flour and salt into a bowl.
2. Rub in butter and lard until the mixture resembles fine breadcrumbs.
3. Add the water gradually, gathering the mixture into a ball. Knead lightly just until it is smooth. Wrap in a plastic bag and allow to rest for 20 minutes in the refrigerator.

Filling
4. Place the eggs in a bowl and beat slightly. Beat in the sugar, nutmeg, milk, and vanilla.
5. Pour into the pastry lined dish.
6. Bake in an oven preheated to 230°C (450°F), or Gas mark 8, for 15 minutes.
7. Reduce the temperature to 170°C (325°F) and bake for a further 25-30 minutes. Sprinkle with extra nutmeg.

Pumpkin Pie

INGREDIENTS
Serves 6

Short Pastry (all-purpose)
240g (2 cups) plain flour
120g (8 Tbsp) butter
15g (1 Tbsp) caster sugar (granulated sugar)
Pinch of salt
75ml (⅓ cup) water

Filling
6 eggs
360g (1 lb) pumpkin
90g (½ cup) sugar
Pinch ground cinnamon
60ml (¼ cup) rum

METHOD

Short Pastry
1. Sieve flour and salt into a bowl. Rub in the butter until the mixture has a texture of bread-crumbs.
2. Add the sugar and water (mixed together). Combine in a soft dough.
3. This short pastry can be made in a food processor.

Filling
1. Peel the pumpkin and cut into 1-2cm (½ inch) dice. Place in a suitable pan with sugar and 2 Tbsp of water.
2. Cover with a lid. Cook gently for 8-12 minutes to produce a purée. Allow to cool.
3. Add eggs, cinnamon, and rum.
4. Line a deep 6-8 inch sponge tin with short pastry.
5. Add the purée, bake in oven 180°C (350°F), Gas mark 4, for 30-40 minutes.
6. Allow to cool. Remove from tin.

This pie goes well with vanilla ice cream.

Apple Pie

Prepare the pastry and line the dish before preparing the apple filling. Once the top pastry has been added to the pie immediately freeze or bake.

INGREDIENTS
Serves 6-8

Pastry
225g (2 cups) plain flour
2ml (½ tsp) salt
110g (8 Tbsp) butter
50g (¼ cup) lard (may subsitute shortening)
15g (1 Tbsp) caster sugar (granulated sugar)
29ml (5 Tbsp) water

Filling
175g (1 cup) caster sugar (granulated sugar)
5ml (1 tsp) cinnamon
450g (1 lb) sliced apples
25g (2 Tbsp) butter

METHOD

Pastry
1. Sift flour, salt, and sugar into a bowl.
2. Rub in butter and lard until the mixture resembles fine breadcrumbs.
3. Add the water gradually, gathering the mix into a ball. Knead lightly just until it is smooth. Wrap in plastic and allow to rest in the refrigerator for 20 minutes.

Filling
1. Line a pie dish with pastry.
2. Mix together the sugar and cinnamon. Toss the sliced apples through the mixture. Place this mixture into the pastry-lined dish and dot with butter.
3. Cover with the top pastry and cut slits in the top.
4. Bake in an oven preheated to 220°C (425°F), Gas mark 7, on the lowest shelf of oven for about 1 hour, or until the pastry is nicely browned.

Bakewell Tart

INGREDIENTS
Serves 4-6

Sweet Short Pastry
120g (1 cup) flour
50g (4 Tbsp) butter
30g (2 Tbsp) sugar
1 small egg
Pinch salt

Frangipane Sponge Mixture
Almond essence, if desired
50g (¼ cup) ground almonds
50g (4 Tbsp) butter
50g (¼ cup) caster sugar (granulated sugar)
1 egg
25g (3 Tbsp) flour

Tart
Raspberry jam
Icing sugar (confectioners sugar)

METHOD

Pastry
1. Sieve flour into a bowl.
2. Rub in butter and pinch of salt until it resembles fine breadcrumbs.
3. Beat egg and sugar together in a bowl.
4. Add beaten egg and sugar to flour and work to a paste.
5. Allow to stand for 20 minutes in a cool place.

Frangipane Sponge Mixture
1. Cream butter and sugar together thoroughly.
2. Beat egg and add little by little to butter and sugar.
3. Fold through sieved flour and almonds.
4. Add essence, if desired.

Bakewell Tart

CONTINUED

Tart
1. Line a 12 cm (6 inch) flan ring with pastry.
2. Spread the base of the pastry with raspberry jam.
3. Fill flan with two-thirds frangipane sponge mixture and decorate the top with strips of pastry.
4. Bake in a moderate oven, 160°C (320°F), Gas mark 3, 45 minutes or until set.
5. Dust with icing sugar to give a glaze.
6. Serve hot with custard or cold with cream.

PUDDINGS

Queen of Puddings

Queen of Puddings

INGREDIENTS
Serves 4

275ml (1¼ cups) milk
110g (1 cup) white bread crumbs or sponge cake crumbs
10g (1 Tbsp) butter
100g (½ cup) caster sugar (granulated sugar), divided
3 eggs, separated
50g (¼ cup) strawberry jam

METHOD

1. Bring the milk to the boil and stir in the bread crumbs or cake crumbs and butter, then leave to stand for 10 minutes.
2. Beat egg yolks with 10g (1 Tbsp) caster sugar and stir into bread crumb or cake crumb mixture.
3. Pour into a greased 1½ pt ovenproof dish.
4. Bake at 160°C (325°F), or Gas mark 3, for 30 minutes, or until set.
5. Remove from oven. Spread with jam.
6. Whisk egg whites until stiff and gradually whisk in remaining sugar a little at a time.
7. Spread meringue over and return to the oven for a further 15 minutes at the same temperature until golden brown.
8. Serve at once.

Mincemeat Roly-Poly

INGREDIENTS
Serves 4-6

Suet Crust Pastry
200g (1⅔ cups) self-raising flour
2ml (½ tsp) salt
90g (½ cup) shredded suet

Filling
90g (½ cup) mincemeat

METHOD

Pastry
1. Half-fill a steamer with water and put it on to boil.
2. Mix together the flour, salt, and suet.
3. Add enough cold water to give a light, elastic dough and knead very lightly until smooth. Roll out to 5mm (¼ inch) thick in an oblong about 23 x 28cm (9 x 11 inch).

Roly-Poly
1. Spread the mincemeat on the pastry. Leave 5mm (½ inch) clear along each edge.
2. Brush the edges with milk and roll the pastry up evenly, starting from one short side.
3. Place the roll on greased foil and wrap the foil round the roll loosely, allowing room for expansion, but seal the edges very well.
4. Steam the roly-poly over rapidly boiling water for 1½-2 hours.
5. When cooked, remove it from the foil and serve with custard.

Suet Puddings

A number of popular sweet and savoury puddings are made either with suet crust pastry or with a somewhat wetter, slacker mixture that is steamed or boiled in a pudding basin or cloth.

INGREDIENTS
Serves 4-6

> 175g (1½ cups) self-raising flour
> Pinch of salt
> 75g (6 Tbsp) shredded suet
> 50g (¼ cup) caster sugar (granulated sugar)
> 150ml (⅔ cup) milk

METHOD

1. Half-fill a steamer or large saucepan with water and put on to boil.
2. Grease a 900ml (2 pt) pudding basin.
3. Mix the flour, salt, suet, and sugar.
4. Make a well in the centre and add enough milk to give a soft dropping consistency.
5. Put into the greased basin, cover with greased greaseproof paper or foil. Secure with string.
6. Steam over rapidly boiling water for 1½-2 hours.
7. Serve with a jam, golden syrup (light corn syrup), custard, or fruit sauce.

Suet Puddings

VARIATIONS

Lighter Pudding
Use 75g (½ cup) self-raising flour and 75g (⅔ cup) fresh breadcrumbs.

Richer Pudding
Use 1 beaten egg and 6 Tbsp milk instead of 150ml (⅔ cup) milk.

Jam
Put 2 Tbsp jam in the bottom of your greased pudding basin before adding the mixture.

Apple
Add to dry ingredients 225g (½ lb) cooked apples. Serve the pudding with a sweet, white sauce flavoured with nutmeg or ground cinnamon.

Rich Fig
Add to dry ingredients 100g (¼ lb) chopped dried figs, 50g (½ cup) chopped, blanched almonds, and the grated rind of 1 lemon. Mix to a soft dropping consistency with 2 beaten eggs and 2 Tbsp sherry or milk. Serve hot with custard.

Apple Suet Pudding

INGREDIENTS
Serves 4-6

Suet Crust Pastry
200g (1⅔ cups) self-raising flour
2ml (½ tsp) salt
90g (½ cup) shredded suet

Filling
450g (1 lb) cooking apples, peeled, cored, and sliced
100g (8 Tbsp) sugar

METHOD

1. Half-fill a steamer or large saucepan with water and put it on to boil.
2. Grease a 900ml (4 cup) pudding basin.
3. Mix together the flour, salt, and suet to make the pastry.
4. Roll out into a round 2.5 cm (1 inch) larger all round than the top of the basin.
5. Cut a quarter out of round. With the remaining portion line the pudding basin, dampening the edges, overlapping them, and pressing well to seal.
6. Fill the basin with sliced apples and sugar in alternating layers.
7. Roll out the remaining pastry to make a lid, damp the edges of the pastry in the basin and cover with lid, pressing the edges well together.
8. Cover with greased greaseproof paper and steam for 2½ hours.

Fruit Suet Puddings

VARIATIONS

Use different fruits, such as rhubarb, plums, damsons (increasing the sugar to 175g (¾ cup)), blackberries combined with apples, or blackcurrants, prepared as for stewing. When the softer fruits are used, steam for only 2 hours.

Steaming times for puddings:
Small pudding: cooked in individual basin 30 minutes–1 hour.
Large pudding: 2-3 hours, according to size.
Meat pudding: 3-4 hours if meat is uncooked.

A suet pudding improves with extra cooking. The result will be unpalatable if it is cooked for too short a time.

Christmas Pudding

You can keep Christmas puddings for a year. The pudding will improve.

INGREDIENTS

Serves 16-20
Makes 1 x 920g (4 lb) pudding, 2 x 900g (2 lb) puddings, or 4 x 450g (1 lb) puddings

300g (1¼ cups) suet
120g (1 cup) flour
50g (½ cup) ground almonds
180g (1½ cups) breadcrumbs
250g (2 cups) sultanas (golden raisins)
240g (1¾ cups) raisins
300g (2¼ cups) currants
60g (¼ cup) chopped peel
180g (1 cup) brown sugar
10g (1 Tbsp) mixed spice (pumpkin pie spices)
5g (1 tsp) salt
150g (⅔ cup) eggs
Zest and juice of 1 lemon
Zest and juice of 1 orange
75ml (⅓ cup) beer or brandy
50ml (¼ cup) milk

METHOD

1. Put all dry ingredients and dried fruits into a large mixing bowl.
2. Blend well together.
3. Mix together zest and juice of lemon and orange, and beer or brandy.
4. Mix well into dry ingredients.
5. Beat egg and milk together and add to mixture.
6. Blend together and rest for one hour.
7. This mix is best left a day before cooking.

Christmas Pudding

CONTINUED

8. Next day fill the mixture to the top of well-greased pudding basins.
9. Cover each basin with two discs of greaseproof paper cut to size.
10. Lay a square of clean cloth over each basin, tie this under the rim with string.
11. Either boil or steam as follows: 4 lb pudding – 8 hours, 2 lb pudding – 6 hours, 1 lb pudding – 4 hours
12. Once started, the pudding must not be allowed to go off the boil.
13. When finished, the pudding should be removed at once from the boiling water or the steamer.
14. Untie cloth and leave extended to dry thoroughly.
15. When the puddings have cooled, remove the cloth leaving the greaseproof discs untouched.
16. Tie up the top again using a clean cloth.
17. Store the pudding in a cool dry place.
18. Serve on Christmas Day with rum or brandy sauce.

Lemon Steamed Sponge Pudding

INGREDIENTS

Serves 4

60g (¼ cup) butter
60g (⅓ cup) sugar
1 egg
120g (1 cup) flour
7g (2 tsp) baking powder
25ml (2 Tbsp) milk
1 lemon, juice and zest
Vanilla essence

METHOD

1. Cream butter and sugar; beat in egg. Fold through sieved flour and baking powder. Add milk to adjust to piping consistency.
2. Add lemon juice, zest, and vanilla.
3. Pipe into buttered ovenproof dish and steam for 45 minutes.

This recipe can be baked in a moderate oven 180°C (350°F) for 30 minutes.

Hot Lemon Sauce

This is nice served with any steamed pudding, and is different from regular custard. It can be made ahead of time and reheated without any problem.

INGREDIENTS

Makes 300ml (1¼ cups)

15g (2 Tbsp) cornflour (cornstarch)
45g (4 Tbsp) caster sugar (granulated sugar), sieved
Juice and finely grated rind of 2 lemons
300ml (1¼ cups) milk, boiled
25g (2 Tbsp) butter, melted
3 egg yolks, gently beaten

METHOD

1. Put the cornflour, sugar, lemon rind, and juice into a Pyrex bowl and beat together.
2. Place the bowl over a pan of simmering water and add the boiled milk and melted butter through a sieve.
3. Beat in the egg yolks and continue to cook over the simmering water for about 10 minutes, stirring occasionally, until the mixture begins to thicken.

Pudding Soufflé Rothschild

INGREDIENTS

Serves 4

> 190ml (¾ cup) milk
> 60g (5 Tbsp) sugar
> Vanilla pod or essence
> 60g (¼ cup) butter
> 60g (½ cup) flour
> 4 eggs, separated
> 30ml (2 Tbsp) Kirsch
> 15g (2 Tbsp) candied fruit

METHOD

1. Boil milk, sugar, and essence and pour into creamed butter and flour.
2. Return to the stove and re-boil.
3. Cool slightly and beat in egg yolks.
4. Fold in stiffly beaten egg whites.
5. Add Kirsch; fold in candied fruit.
6. Fill buttered and sugared moulds two-thirds full.
7. Cook in a bain-marie (water in a tray) for 20 minutes in a moderate oven, 180°C (350°F), Gas mark 4.
8. Serve immediately.

Passion Fruit Soufflé

INGREDIENTS

Serves 4

Passion fruit
2 egg whites
75g (6 Tbsp) sugar

METHOD

1. Take several large passion fruit, cut in half and scoop out the contents.
2. Place in a saucepan and simmer to a syrup, stirring all the time. Remove from heat, allow to cool.
3. Whisk the egg whites slowly, adding the sugar, until firm.
4. Fold in sufficient passion fruit syrup to give a strong flavour but without thinning the whites too much.
5. Butter 4 ramekins, add a couple of tsps of passion fruit syrup to the bottom. Fill with meringue mix proud of the ramekin (filling above the top rim of the ramekin).
6. Bake in a hot oven till well risen and golden (5-8 mins).

These soufflés can be kept in the fridge when cooked as above and then reheated in a hot oven and will once again rise superbly.

Sweet Soufflé Omelette

INGREDIENTS
Serves 2-4

2 eggs
5ml (1 tsp) caster sugar (granulated sugar)
30ml (2 Tbsp) water
Knob (2 Tbsp, more or less) of butter

METHOD

1. Separate the yolks from the egg whites of the eggs, putting them in different bowls.
2. Whisk the yolks until creamy.
3. Add the sugar and water and beat again.
4. Whisk the egg whites until stiff, but not dry.
5. At this point place the oven-proof omelette pan containing the butter over a low heat and let the butter melt without browning.
6. Turn the egg whites into the yolk mixture and fold in carefully, using a spoon.
7. Grease the sides of the pan with butter by tilting it in all directions, and then pour in the egg mixture.
8. Cook over a moderate heat until the omelette is golden brown on the underside.
9. Put under the grill (broiler) until the omelette is golden brown on top.
10. Remove at once as overcooking tends to make it tough.
11. Run a spatula gently round the edge and underneath the omelette to loosen it, make a mark across the middle at right angles to the pan handle, add any required filling and double the omelette over.
12. Turn it gently on to a hot plate and serve at once.

Sweet Soufflé Omelette

FILLINGS

Jam
Spread the cooked omelette with warm jam, fold it over and sprinkle with caster sugar.

Rum
1 Tbsp of rum added to eggs, (but only use 1 Tbsp of water added to the egg yolks before cooking.) Put the cooked omelette on a hot dish, pour over 3-4 Tbsp of warmed rum round it, ignite and serve immediately.

Apricot
Add the grated rind of an orange or tangerine to the egg yolks. Spread some thick apricot pulp over the omelette before folding it and serve sprinkled with caster sugar.

Saxone Pudding Soufflé

INGREDIENTS

Serves 4

190ml (¾ cup) milk
60g (5 Tbsp) sugar
Vanilla pod or essence
60g (¼ cup) butter
60g (½ cup) flour
4 eggs, separated
1 lemon

METHOD

1. Boil milk, sugar, and essence and pour into creamed butter and flour.
2. Return to the stove and re-boil.
3. Cool slightly and beat in egg yolks.
4. Fold in stiffly beaten egg whites.
5. Add juice and zest of lemon.
6. Fill buttered and sugared moulds two-thirds full.
7. Cook in a bain-marie (water in a tray) for 20 minutes in a moderate oven, 180°C (350°F), Gas mark 4.
8. Serve immediately.

Baked Soufflé Omelette

INGREDIENTS

Serves 2-4

> 4 eggs
> 28g (2 Tbsp) caster sugar (granulated sugar)
> 6 almonds, blanched and finely chopped
> 30ml (2 Tbsp) water
> Pinch salt
> Knob (2 Tbsp, more or less) of butter
> Sugar for dredging
> Jam or stewed fruit, optional

METHOD

1. Separate the yolks from the white of the eggs, and whisk the yolks thoroughly with the sugar.
2. Add the almonds and the water.
3. Whisk the egg whites and the salt stiffly and fold into the yolk mixture.
4. Grease a shallow ovenproof dish with butter and put the omelette mixture into it.
5. Bake in a moderate oven, 180°C (350°F), Gas mark 4, for 15-20 minutes. Sprinkle with sugar and serve at once.
6. A little jam or some stewed fruit may be put at the bottom of the dish before the egg mixture is added.

Crème Brûlée

INGREDIENTS

Serves 8

4 egg yolks
28g (2 Tbsp) caster sugar (granulated sugar)
600ml (2¼ cups) double cream (whipping cream)
Vanilla pod or 5ml (¼ tsp) vanilla essence
113g (½ cup) Demerara sugar (natural brown sugar)

METHOD

1. Combine the egg yolks and caster sugar and whisk until the mixture is pale and fluffy.
2. Put the cream in a pan with the vanilla pod and bring slowly to the boil. Fish out the vanilla pod (wash and dry the pod, which will live to serve another day).
3. If using vanilla essence, add it after the cream has boiled and cooled a little.
4. Whisk the cream into the egg mixture. Rinse the pan and strain the custard into it through a fine sieve.
5. Heat gently, stirring constantly (do not allow the mixture to boil) until it will coat the back of a wooden spoon.
6. Pour the custard into eight or more small ramekins, filling them almost to the brim.
7. Stand the ramekins in an ovenproof tin and pour in boiling water to come halfway up their sides.
8. Bake in a very cool oven, 120°C (250°F), Gas mark ½, for about 40 minutes, or until the custard is set firm.
9. Allow them to cool, then chill them for at least four hours.
10. To caramelise the tops, sprinkle with Demerara sugar, put under grill (broiler) until sugar melts and bubbles.
11. Cool quickly and chill again before serving.

Chocolate and Rum Roulade

Roulade is from the French word "rouler" meaning "to roll."

INGREDIENTS
Serves 6-8

Melted butter
6 eggs, separated
175g (1 cup) caster sugar (granulated sugar)
755g (1⅔ lb) good plain chocolate, broken into pieces
45ml (3 Tbsp) dark rum

Filling
450ml (2 cups) double cream (whipping cream)
45g (¼ cup) caster sugar (granulated sugar)
45ml (3 Tbsp) dark rum

METHOD

1. You will need a shallow sided tin measuring about 28 x 35cm (11 x 14 inch) and this will need to be lined with silicone (parchment) paper.
2. Grease this well with melted butter.
3. Pre-heat the oven to Gas mark 4, 180°C (350°F), and try to double-check the temperature if you can. Even the slightest variation in temperature can be disastrous when baking roulades. Use an oven thermometer if you have one.

Roulade Mixture
1. Put the egg yolks in a warmed bowl and beat them to a ribbon stage for at least 5 minutes until white and light.
2. Then, little by little, beat in the sugar.
3. The whole process should take at least 12 minutes.
4. In a double saucepan, for this particular roulade, melt the chocolate pieces with the rum. Leave to cool fractionally.
5. Meanwhile, begin to beat the egg whites in a mixing bowl – you want them to be stiff.

Continued

Chocolate and Rum Roulade

CONTINUED

6. Transfer the egg yolk and sugar mixture to a large plastic bowl and pour the melted, cooled chocolate in through a sieve.
7. Fold in well. (For the other roulades below, fold in dry flavouring ingredients at this stage).
8. Fold in one-third of the stiffly beaten egg whites, then beat the remainder of the egg whites back to a stiff consistency (they can flop quite quickly).
9. Fold these in, using a long-handled metal spoon.
10. Turn the mixture out into the buttered, paper-lined tray. Spread evenly across and into the corners without pushing.

Baking the Roulade
1. Place the filled tray in the carefully pre-heated oven and bake for 20-30 minutes. To ensure that it is ready, bring the tray gently halfway out of the oven and insert a thin skewer in the middle.
2. If the roulade is cooked the skewer should come out completely dry. The top should be crisp and cracky too.
3. Take the roulade out of the oven when it is ready and cover the top with a clean, dry tea towel.
4. Cover this in turn with a well dampened tea towel, and you will see the steam rise. This settles the crisp top, and will make the roulade easier to roll when it is cool.
5. Leave to cool in the tin, preferably overnight.

Turning out
1. Cover a wooden board larger than the roulade tin with foil and then a double thickness of good greaseproof paper.
2. Put this board, papered side towards the roulade, on top of the roulade tin, and invert the tin on to the board. The roulade will come out, its paper casing on the top.
3. You need now to remove this paper casing, but don't do it in one fell swoop as you might tear bits of the cake away.

Chocolate and Rum Roulade

CONTINUED

4. Lay one hand on the paper towards one end of the roulade and tear the paper off in strips. It takes longer but better to be safe than sorry.

Filling and Rolling
1. You can really use anything you fancy to fill a roulade, but the simplest, often the most delicious, filling is whipped flavoured cream.
2. Whip the cream up with the sugar and alcohol and then spread over the whole roulade surface.
3. To roll, start at the long end nearest you and, lifting the ends of the double sheets of greaseproof paper and foil the roulade is resting on, give the roulade a little push away from you. Carry on pushing and it should roll well.

Finish
1. Cut off about 2.5cm (1 inch) at each end of the roulade to neaten, and then carefully lift-you'll need two fish slicers (2 wide knives) or an extra pair of hands-on to a serving platter.
2. Sprinkle with icing sugar for that final touch.

This is an excellent sweet and well worth all the effort.

Variations of Roulade
1. Chocolate and Brandy: Simply replace the rum in the basic recipe with brandy. This is rather good at Christmas.
2. Coffee and Hazelnut: Instead of chocolate and rum, fold into the beaten egg yolks 100g (1 cup) ground hazelnuts mixed with 2 level Tbsp powdered Nescafé coffee.
3. Mango and Coconut: Instead of the chocolate and rum, fold into the beaten egg yolks 100g (1 cup) toasted, desiccated (dried) coconut with 1 fresh mango, peeled and then the flesh coarsely grated.

Lemon Cheese Crisp Cheesecake

INGREDIENTS

Serves 6

Base
200g (1⅔ cups) digestive biscuits, crushed into crumbs (may substitute graham crackers)
110g (½ cup) butter, softened
25g (2 Tbsp) caster sugar (granulated sugar)

Filling
150g (6 oz) cream cheese, softened
1 tin (14 oz) condensed milk (sweetened condensed milk)
100ml (½ cup) freshly squeezed lemon juice, strained

METHOD

Base
1. Cream butter and sugar. Add biscuit crumbs.
2. Beat together until well blended.
3. Press down into 20cm (8 inch) flan tin.

Filling
1. Beat all ingredients until the lumps have disappeared and the texture is like cream.
2. Pour over biscuit base and put in fridge to chill until needed.
3. Decorate with lemon slices.

Blender Cheesecake

INGREDIENTS
Serves 8

Base
275g (10oz/2½ cups) packet chocolate digestive biscuits
    (may substitute chocolate graham crackers)
50g (¼ cup) butter, melted

Filling *(double filling recipe for flavored fillings)*
15g (4 Tbsp) powdered gelatine or leaf gelatine
75ml (⅓ cup) alcohol (see next page)
250g (8 oz) good cream cheese
2 whole eggs
2 egg yolks
50g (¼ cup) caster sugar (granulated sugar)
300ml (1¼ cups) double cream (whipping cream)
Flavouring of your choice (see next page)

METHOD

Base
1. Pre-heat the oven to 180°C (350°F), Gas mark 4. Line a 10 inch loose-bottomed cake tin (springform pan) with greaseproof paper.
2. For the base, drop the biscuits in pieces in to your liquidiser and reduce to fine crumbs.
3. Turn out into mixing bowl, add melted butter and mix well to a paste.
4. Press this onto the bottom of prepared tin and bake in the oven for 15 minutes.
5. Remove and leave to cool. The cooling is most important before adding the cheesecake mixture.

Filling
1. First of all, put the gelatine into a small saucepan, and, all in one go pour in 75ml (⅓ cup) alcohol chosen for desired flavouring. (See page 125).
2. Gently swirl the pan around until the fine particles dissolve and become rather tacky; put to one side and leave until reconstitution time comes around.

Continued

Blender Cheesecake

CONTINUED

3. Put the cream cheese, eggs and yolks, sugar, and cream into the food processor with the flavouring of your choice (see next page) and mix to a cream.
4. To reconstitute the gelatine, put the gelatine pan on the very lowest heat possible. Keep feeling the bottom of the pan with your hand; it shouldn't hurt, that's how low!
5. The gelatine will be a clear liquid, and then you pour or dribble it into your mixture through a warmed metal sieve. For this blender cheesecake, dribble the gelatine into the blender while it is going. For non-blender gelatine mixtures, fold the gelatine in well, using a long-handled spoon.
6. Pour the first cheesecake mix into the paper and biscuit lined tin, and leave to set.
7. Make up the second mix and pour on top of first.
8. Most dishes with gelatine require 6-8 hours in the fridge.
9. Garnish the cheesecake after taking out of tin with twirls of cream and, or some appropriate fruits.

This blender mix is much denser than the norm. Use two times the filling quantity above, flavouring them differently according to your choice from the alternatives on the next page, placing one on top of the other. So to make one cheesecake, you'll need 500g (1 lb) cream cheese, etc.

Blender Cheesecake

FLAVOURINGS

Strawberry
225g (8 oz/1½ cups) strawberries, hulled, and reconstitute the gelatine with 75ml (⅓ cup) brandy.

Raspberry
225g (8 oz/1½ cups) raspberries, hulled, and reconstitute the gelatine with 75ml (⅓ cup) Kirsch.

Coffee and Rum
Use 2 Tbsps Camp coffee and reconstitute the gelatine with 75ml (⅓ cup) dark rum. If you like, you can add 100g (1 cup) chopped pecan nuts.

Orange Hazelnut
Use the juice and finely grated rind of 2 oranges, and 75g (¾ cup) ground hazelnuts. Reconstitute the gelatine with 75ml (⅓ cup) orange curaçao.

Lemon
Use the juice and finely grated rind of 2 lemons, and reconstitute the gelatine with 75ml (⅓ cup) with gin.

Chocolate
Use 150g (6 oz) good chocolate melted with 2 Tbsp rum, and reconstitute the gelatine with 75ml (⅓ cup) rum.

Orange Sponge Soufflé

INGREDIENTS

Serves 4-6

> 75g (6 Tbsp) butter
> 350g (1¾ cups) caster sugar (granulated sugar)
> 175g (1½ cups) self-raising flour
> 6 eggs, separated
> 275ml (1¼ cups) milk
> 3 oranges, rind and juice
> 55ml (¼ cup) liqueur (Cointreau, Grand Marnier, or Southern Comfort)

METHOD

1. Cream the butter, sugar, flour, and egg yolks together until well blended.
2. Slowly add the milk, beating all the time. Add orange rind and juice and the liqueur of your choice. Mix well.
3. Fold in the stiffly beaten egg whites until evenly blended.
4. Pour into a greased soufflé dish and bake at approximately 180°C (350°F), Gas mark 4, for about 20-25 minutes.
5. Serve immediately.

The sponge rises to the top, leaving a delicious sauce at the bottom. Serve with cream or vanilla ice cream.

Hot Lemon or Orange Soufflé

INGREDIENTS
Serves 6

50g (4 Tbsp) butter
50g (6½ Tbsp) plain flour
275ml (1¼ cups) hot milk
Pinch of salt
1 large lemon or orange, rind and juice
6 eggs, separated
75g (6 Tbsp) caster sugar (granulated sugar)

METHOD

1. Butter a 2 pt soufflé dish and sprinkle the inside with caster sugar.
2. Melt the butter in a saucepan. Stir in the flour and cook for about 1-2 minutes, stirring all the time.
3. Remove the pan from the heat and gradually add the milk and the salt until you have a smooth sauce.
4. Return the pan to the heat and cook, stirring all the time, until the sauce thickens.
5. Remove from the heat and add grated rind and juice.
6. Beat egg yolks well with the sugar and stir into the sauce.
7. Whisk the egg whites until firm but not dry, and fold into the sauce, using a metal spoon.
8. Pour into the prepared dish and bake at approximately 180°C (350°F), Gas mark 4, for 35 minutes or until golden and well risen.
9. Serve at once.

Real Ice Cream

INGREDIENTS

Serves 8

4 eggs, separated
110g (½ cup) caster sugar (granulated sugar)
570ml (2½ cups) double cream (whipping cream), whipped

METHOD

1. Beat the egg yolks and sugar together until quite thick.
2. Stir in the cream until evenly blended and then fold in the stiffly beaten egg whites.
3. Put into 1l (2 pt) polythene (plastic) container and seal.
4. Place in the freezer and leave for 4-5 hours.

This ice cream does not require to be stirred while freezing.

American Ice Cream

INGREDIENTS

Serves 4-6

250ml (1 cup) milk, boiled
250ml (1 cup) cream
½ tin (14 oz) condensed milk (sweetened condensed milk)
1 sheet gelatine
180g (1 cup) sugar
Vanilla essence

METHOD

1. Dissolve gelatine and sugar in milk.
2. Add essence, strain and cool.
3. Add remaining ingredients and freeze.

You can use 1 tsp powdered gelatine for the sheet gelatine; soften in ¼ cup of the cream and add to the hot milk.

Vanilla Ice-cream (English)

INGREDIENTS

Serves 4-6

> 500ml (2¼ cups) milk
> Vanilla essence or vanilla pod
> 4 egg yolks
> 90g (½ cup) sugar

METHOD

1. Bring milk and vanilla essence or pod to the boil.
2. Stir in yolks and sugar. Return to the stove and cook, stirring constantly, until mixture coats the back of a wooden spoon.
3. Strain, cool, and freeze.

Coffee ice: add strong coffee to the mixture.

Chocolate ice: add 120g (4 oz) grated chocolate to milk before boiling.

Strawberry or raspberry ices may be made by flavouring with fruit pulp or purée.

Use pasteurized eggs where possible.

Rhubarb Crumble

INGREDIENTS

Serves 4-6

900g (2 lb) rhubarb
170g (1 cup) brown sugar, divided
Grated zest of 1 orange
170g (1⅓ cups) plain white flour or wholewheat flour
85g (⅓ cup) butter

METHOD

1. Wash and dry the rhubarb.
2. Trim the ends of the stalks and cut them into 2.5cm (1 inch) lengths.
3. Put them in a pie dish and sprinkle with half the sugar and the orange zest.
4. Sift the flour into a bowl; cut the butter into small dice and rub into the flour until the mixture has the texture of fine breadcrumbs.
5. Stir in all but a Tbsp of the remaining sugar.
6. Spoon the crumble mixture over the rhubarb and press it down lightly.
7. Sprinkle the remaining Tbsp of sugar over the top.
8. Bake in a preheated oven 200°C (400°F), Gas mark 6, for 45 minutes to one hour. Serve hot with custard.

Bread and Butter Pudding

INGREDIENTS
Serves 4

450ml (2 cups) milk and cream (half and half)
60g (5 Tbsp) caster sugar (granulated sugar)
3 eggs
2-3 drops vanilla essence
110g (¾ cup) sultanas (golden raisins)
4 slices bread
40g (3 Tbsp) butter
Grated nutmeg

METHOD

1. Place milk and cream (half and half) on to boil, and meanwhile mix the eggs, sugar, and vanilla essence together in a bowl.
2. When the milk and cream has boiled, whisk it into the egg mixture.
3. Strain and put to one side.
4. Butter the bread and cut in half diagonally.
5. Place half the slices of bread and butter in an oven-to-table dish.
6. Sprinkle on the sultanas. Place on the remaining half of the bread.
7. Carefully pour the egg custard over the bread. Sprinkle with nutmeg.
8. Place the dish in a tray of water and bake in the oven, 135°C (275°F), Gas mark 2, for 45 minutes to one hour.

The custard should be firm, not runny. This is a classic English sweet that can be served hot or cold. If cold, a little cream with it is superb. The bread used can vary, for example fruit bread, brioche, etc.

Brandy Snaps

INGREDIENTS

Makes 3 Dozen

135g (2/3 cup) butter
240g (1¼ cups) caster sugar (granulated sugar)
120g (1 cup) soft flour (cake or pastry flour)
120g (½ cup) golden syrup (light corn syrup)
4g (1 tsp) ground ginger

METHOD

1. Mix all the ingredients to a smooth paste.
2. Prepare a baking tin by thorough cleaning and giving it a liberal dressing of oil.
3. Roll out the paste into a long rope and, with a knife, chop off small pieces of equal size (approx 15g or 1 Tbsp). Place these about 13 cm (5 inch) apart on the greased tray and flatten them with the hand.
4. Bake at 170°C (325°F), Gas mark 2, until they are golden in colour.
5. During baking the paste flows out flat with a holey surface.
6. Once they are baked, allow them to cool slightly and then lift them off with a palette knife.
7. Whilst still warm, the brandy snaps may be rolled round a wooden spoon and moulded into shape.
8. When cooled they can be filled with fresh whipped cream, or can be used with many sweets and ice cream.

CAKES

Old-Fashioned Parkin

Old-Fashioned Parkin

INGREDIENTS
Serves 4-6

125g (1 cup) plain flour
2ml (½ tsp) ground cinnamon
7ml (1½ tsp) ground ginger
5ml (1 tsp) bicarbonate of soda (baking soda)
225g (1½ cups) medium oatmeal
50g (¼ cup) butter
25g (2 Tbsp) lard (may subsitute shortening)
225g (⅔ cup) black treacle (molasses)
225g (1 cup) soft brown sugar, packed
1 egg beaten
80ml (⅓ cup) milk

METHOD

1. First, line a square tin about 20cm (8 inch) with greased greaseproof paper. Then sieve together the flour, cinnamon, ginger, and bicarbonate of soda. Add oatmeal, mixing well.
2. Heat together the butter, lard, treacle, and sugar slowly, stirring well, and add it alternately to the flour mixture with the beaten egg. Finally, add the milk and mix to form a fairly soft dough. Turn into the prepared tin and smooth the top over.
3. Bake at 150°C (300°F) or Gas mark 3 for 50-60 minutes.
4. Leave to cool. Cut into squares.

Rich Christmas Cake

INGREDIENTS

Serves 4-6

340g (1¾ cups) butter
340g (2¾ cups) plain flour
340g (1¾ cups) caster sugar (granulated sugar)
500g (3¾ cups) raisins
500g (3¾ cups) currants
115g (¾ cup) mixed peel (zested lemon and orange peel)
177ml (¾ cup) wine or brandy
7 eggs
15g (1 Tbsp) mixed spice

METHOD

1. Beat the butter to a cream. Add sugar then eggs and beat well.
2. Add flour slowly until well mixed.
3. Add the remainder of the ingredients in small quantities. When well mixed turn into a tin lined with baking paper. Put in the oven 150-160°C (300-320°F), moderate, for 3½-4 hours.

The cake rises very little, so the cake should be made nearly as deep as you want it to be. It is improved by keeping it a few weeks before eating.

Pancakes

INGREDIENTS

Serves 8

240g (2 cups) flour
2 eggs
25g (2 Tbsp) butter
Pinch of salt
570ml (2½ cups) milk
120g (½ cup) lard or oil

METHOD

1. Whisk the eggs, salt, and milk together.
2. Add the sieved flour a little at a time, whisking each portion into the liquid to make a smooth batter.
3. Mix in the melted butter.
4. Place a small quantity of lard or oil in a clean, small frying pan and heat to smoking point.
5. Pour in sufficient batter to just cover the base of the pan very thinly.
6. Cook until it is a light golden brown.
7. Turn the pancake over and cook this side to the same colour.
8. Serve with lemon and sugar.

Pancakes

VARIETIES

Jam Pancakes
Basic pancakes, prepared
50g (¼ cup) caster sugar (granulated sugar)
120g (½ cup) jam

1. Spread a spoonful of jam on each pancake.
2. Roll up the pancakes
3. Sprinkle with sugar and serve.

Apple pancakes
Basic pancakes, prepared
4 apples, puréed
120g (½ cup) caster sugar (granulated sugar)

1. Spread each pancake with apple purée.
2. Roll up the pancakes.
3. Sprinkle with sugar and serve.

Crêpe Suzettes
Basic pancakes, prepared
60g (4 Tbsp) butter
60g (¼ cup) sugar
Zest and juice of 1 orange
30g (2 Tbsp) Grand Marnier
30g (2 Tbsp) Cognac

1. Zest and juice the orange into a bowl.
2. Add the sugar and Grand Marnier and stir to dissolve.
3. Place the butter in a hot pan and when melted, add the liqueur mixture.
4. Place the pancakes in the pan one at a time, covering it with the sauce and folding into fourths.
5. Pour the brandy over the pancakes and light by holding the pan sideways over a gas flame.
6. Serve immediately with the sauce.

Crepes Rothschild

INGREDIENTS

Serves 4-6

.5l (2 cups) milk
100g (½ cup) sugar
125g (1 cup) flour
125g (½ cup) butter
Vanilla essence
6 eggs
Apricot jam
Heavy cream
Icing sugar (confectioners sugar)

METHOD

1. Put milk, sugar, flour, butter, and vanilla essence in a saucepan. Cook until the mixture thickens, stirring all the time.
2. Add the egg yolks to the mixture.
3. Whip the egg whites and fold in to the mixture.
4. Line a baking sheet with parchment. Form 13cm (5 inch). pancakes, and bake in a hot oven (450°F) for 5 minutes.
5. Place a spoon of apricot jam in the centre. Add a spoon of extra thick cream, dust with icing sugar, and serve.

David's Carrot Cake

This cake, sometimes known as passion cake, traditionally has a cream cheese icing, but I prefer to use low-fat curd cheese, which is less fatty.

INGREDIENTS
Serves 4-6

110g (½ cup) sugar
110g (½ cup) butter
2 eggs
30g (1½ Tbsp) black treacle (molasses)
2ml (½ tsp) baking powder
175g (1½ cups) self-raising flour
1 tsp cinnamon
175g (6oz-1 cup) carrots, finely grated
50g (½ cup) walnuts, finely chopped

Icing
175g (¾ cup) low-fat curd cheese
    (may substitute cottage cheese)
50g (¼ cup) butter
175g (1½ cups) icing sugar (confectioners sugar)

METHOD

1. Grease and flour a 20.5cm (8 inch) ring mould.
2. Beat the sugar and butter together and add the eggs and treacle.
3. Sift the flour, baking powder, and cinnamon.
4. Fold into the mixture. Stir in the carrots and nuts.
5. Bake at 180°C (350°F), Gas mark 4, for 1 hour.
   Icing
6. Beat together the cheese and butter.
7. Add the icing sugar and beat until smooth.
8. Spread over the top of the cooled cake.

David's Fat Free Fruit Loaf

INGREDIENTS

Serves 4-6

700g (4½ cups) mixed dried fruit
570ml (2⅔ cups) cold tea
225g (1 cup) brown sugar
450g (3⅔ cups) self-raising flour
1 egg

METHOD

1. Soak the fruit and sugar in the tea overnight.
2. Next day gradually stir in the flour and egg.
3. Grease a 2 lb loaf tin.
4. Turn mixture into tin and bake in centre of oven at 180°C (350°F), Gas mark 4, for 1¼ to 1½ hours.

Gingerbread

David's Grandma's Recipe

INGREDIENTS

Serves 4-6

    450g (3⅔ cups) flour
    110g (½ cup) butter
    2ml (½ tsp) baking powder
    110g (9 Tbsp) sugar
    110g (¾ cup) cherries
    2ml (½ tsp) salt
    110g (½ cup) chopped stem ginger (preserved ginger:
        fresh ginger that has been preserved in sugar syrup)
    75g (½ cup) mixed peel (zested lemon and orange peel)
    110g (¾ cup) raisins
    350g (1 cup) treacle (molasses)
    275ml (1¼ cups) milk
    2ml (½ tsp) bicarbonate of soda (baking soda)

METHOD

1. Rub the fat into the flour and add the dry ingredients except the soda.
2. Stir in the treacle, slightly warmed.
3. Warm the milk, add to the bicarbonate of soda, and stir well into the mixture.
4. Pour into a well-greased tin and bake in a slow oven for about 1¼ hours at 150°C (300°F), Gas mark 2.

Milk Chocolate Cake

INGREDIENTS

Serves 4-6

Cake
200g (1⅔ cups) self-raising flour
25g (3 Tbsp) cocoa
225g (1⅛ cups) caster sugar (granulated sugar)
2ml (½ tsp) salt
110g (½ cup) butter
2 eggs, beaten
75g (⅓ cup) evaporated milk
75g (⅓ cup) water
5ml (1 tsp) vanilla essence

Filling
110g (½ cup) butter
110g (1 cup) icing sugar (confectioners sugar)
45g (3 Tbsp) strong black coffee

Icing
110g (1 cup) icing sugar
45g (3 Tbsp) strong black coffee
1 milk chocolate Flake

METHOD

Cake
1. Line and grease two 8 inch sponge sandwich tins.
2. Sieve flour and cocoa together into a mixing bowl.
3. Stir in sugar and salt, then rub in butter. Stir in eggs, milk, water, and essence.
4. When smooth divide mixture equally between the tins.
5. Bake at approximately 180°C (350°F), Gas mark 4, on the middle shelf for about 35 minutes, until the cakes have shrunk from the sides of the tins and spring back when touched.
6. Remove from the oven and allow to cool on a wire cooling tray.

Milk Chocolate Cake

CONTINUED

Filling
1. Beat the butter for the filling until smooth and fluffy.
2. Add the sieved icing sugar and coffee and beat again.
3. Spread the filling on the inside of both the cakes and press together.

Icing
1. Sieve the icing sugar into a basin and stir in sufficient coffee to make a smooth icing.
2. Spread over the top of the cake and decorate by crumbling the Flake over the icing.

(The chocolate Flake is an English candy bar that crumbles easily; if unavailable, grate a chocolate bar to use as a garnish.)

Chocolate Brownies

Delia's advice on making brownies is that they are meant to be soft and squidgy in the middle.

INGREDIENTS
Serves 4-6

- 50g (2 oz) dark chocolate, 75% cocoa solids
- 110g (½ cup) butter
- 2 large eggs, beaten
- 225g (1⅛ cups) granulated sugar
- 50g (½ cup) plain flour
- 5ml (1 tsp) baking powder
- Good pinch of salt
- 225g (¾ cup) chocolate chips

METHOD

1. Pre-heat the oven to 180°C (350°F), Gas mark 4. Grease and line an 8 inch square baking tin.
2. Melt the chocolate and butter together in a bowl over a pan of barely simmering water, taking care not to let the bottom of the bowl touch the water. Beat until smooth.
3. Add the remaining ingredients and stir until completely blended. Pour into the prepared tin and bake for 30 minutes until the top looks dry and slightly springy in the centre. Leave to cool in the tin for at least 30 minutes.

American Doughnuts

INGREDIENTS

Serves 12

> 240g (2 cups) strong (bread) flour
> 10g (2 tsp) fresh yeast
> 125ml (½ cup) milk and water, mixed
> 1 egg
> 60g (¼ cup) butter
> 30g (2 Tbsp) caster sugar (granulated sugar)
> Oil for frying

METHOD

1. Sieve the flour into a bowl and warm. Flour should be room temperature or warmer.
2. Dissolve the yeast in a basin with a little of the liquid.
3. Make a well in the centre of the flour.
4. Add the dissolved yeast and sprinkle with a little water. Cover with a tea towel, and leave in a warm place until the yeast bubbles.
5. Add the beaten egg, butter, sugar, and remainder of liquid. Knead well to form a soft, slack, smooth dough, free from stickiness.
6. Keep covered and allow to proof in a warm place.
7. Pin out to 1.5cm (¼ inch) thickness and cut into rings using two cutters, 7.5cm (3 inch) and 4cm (1½ inch).
8. Deep fry to gold brown and toss in sugar.

Nice hot or cold.

Lavender Shortbread

INGREDIENTS
Serves 4-6

350g (2¾ cups) plain flour
350g (1½ cups) good unsalted butter
150g (1 cup) cornflour (cornstarch)
175g (¾ cup + 2 Tbsp) caster sugar (granulated sugar)
Fresh new lavender heads only – strip off the flowers about 225g (2 cups)

METHOD

1. Put all dry ingredients into a mixing bowl and rub in the butter to a fine crumb.
2. When sticky and fine, add the lavender.
3. Stir well.
4. Press into swiss roll tin or similar and prick with a fork all over.
5. Bake in a medium-hot oven, 200°C (400°F), or Gas mark 6, for 35-45 minutes until golden brown.
6. Slice into fingers.

By kind permission of Mr and Mrs Peter Harris.

David's Shortbread

INGREDIENTS

Serves 4-6

    225g (1¾ cups) plain flour
    110g (¾ cup + 2 Tbsp) cornflour (cornstarch)
    110g (½ cup) caster sugar (granulated sugar)
    225g (1 cup) butter, softened

METHOD

1. Sieve the flours together. Rub in the butter to a fine crumb and stir in the caster sugar. Knead together to form a ball. Divide into two and shape into flat rounds.

2. Mark round the edge with your thumb and prick the middle with a fork. Bake on a greased and floured baking sheet at 170°C (325°F), Gas mark 3, 140°C in a fan oven (300°F in a convection oven), for approximately 30 minutes.

Millionaire's Shortbread

Queen Mother's recipe from Windsor Royal Lodge given by the Queen Mother's cook to David.

INGREDIENTS
Serves 4-6

Shortbread
225g (1¾ cups) plain flour
110g (1 cup) icing sugar (confectioners sugar)
110g (¾ cup + 2 Tbsp) cornflour (cornstarch)
225g (1 cup) butter

Toffee
1 can condensed milk (sweetened condensed milk)
225g (1 cup) butter
55ml (¼ cup) golden syrup (light corn syrup)
225g (1 cup + 2 Tbsp) caster sugar (granulated sugar)
225g (8 oz) chocolate, melted

METHOD

Shortbread
1. Blend together all ingredients to make a smooth paste.
2. Roll out to 2cm (¾ inch) thick, put on a baking sheet and cook in a low oven, 150°C (300°F), Gas mark 2, for 30 minutes or until it is just about to go a pale brown colour.
3. Take out and cool.

Toffee
1. Put all the ingredients (except the chocolate) in a thick saucepan and cook slowly until it turns to a nice toffee brown.
2. Melt 225g (8 oz) chocolate in a bowl over a pan of hot water.
3. Cover the cooled shortbread with toffee and put in a cool place for 20 minutes.
4. Pour melted chocolate over toffee. Leave to cool, then cut up into pieces.

BISCUITS & SCONES

Almond Lace Biscuits

Almond Lace Biscuits (Cookies)

INGREDIENTS
Serves 4-6

50g (¼ cup) butter
50g (½ cup) icing sugar (confectioners sugar)
15g (2 Tbsp) plain flour
50g (½ cup) flaked almonds, roughly chopped
1 grated orange zest

METHOD

1. Cream the butter, icing sugar, and orange zest until pale in colour.
2. Add the flour and the almonds and mix well.
3. Line a baking tray with parchment.
4. Place 1 tsp of mixture on the tray, leaving room to spread. Flatten to the size of a 10p coin (quarter). Bake in a hot oven (450°F) for 5-6 minutes.
5. Remove and place over a rolling pin to cool, or allow to cool flat on the parchment.

American Biscuits (Cookies)

These are easy to make and taste delicious.

INGREDIENTS
Serves 12

> 175g (¾ cup) butter or margarine
> 50g (¼ cup) sugar
> 175g (1½ cups) self-raising flour
> 50g (¼ cup) custard powder

METHOD

1. Cream the butter or margarine with the sugar.
2. Sift the flour and custard powder together, then add to the creamed mixture a little at a time.
3. Roll the dough into little balls. Roll each ball in sugar and place on a greased baking tray. Flatten with a fork.
4. Bake in a moderate oven, 180°C (350°F), Gas mark 4, until golden brown, about 10 minutes.

Cheese Scone Round

INGREDIENTS

Serves 4-6

> 225g (2 cups) self-raising flour
> 2ml (½ tsp) salt
> 2ml (½ tsp) mustard powder (ground mustard)
> 5ml (1 tsp) baking powder
> 25g (2 Tbsp) butter
> 175g (1¾ cups) matured cheddar (sharp cheddar), grated
> 1 egg
> 55ml (¼ cup) milk

METHOD

1. Sieve flour, salt, baking powder, and mustard powder.
2. Rub in butter to a fine, sandy texture.
3. Mix egg and milk together. Make a bay in the dry ingredients and add liquid.
4. Add grated cheese.
5. Mix thoroughly to a smooth texture.
6. Turn out on to a floured board, roll out to 2cm (¾ inch) thickness. Cut in rounds and brush with milk.
7. Place on a greased baking tray near the top of the oven and bake in a hot oven, Gas mark 7, 220°C (450°F), for 10-12 minutes.

Plain Scones

INGREDIENTS

Serves 4-6

225g (2 cups) self-raising flour
10ml (2 tsp) baking powder
50g (¼ cup) butter
25g (2 Tbsp) caster sugar (granulated sugar)
55ml (¼ cup) milk
1 egg

METHOD

1. Sieve flour and baking powder.
2. Rub in butter to a fine, sandy texture
3. Mix egg and milk together and add the sugar.
4. Make a bay in the dry ingredients and add the liquid.
5. Mix thoroughly to a smooth texture.
6. Turn out on to a floured board, roll out to 2cm (¾ inch) thickness. Cut in rounds and brush with milk.
7. Place on a greased baking tray and bake in a hot oven, Gas mark 7, 220°C (450°F), for 10-12 minutes, near to the top of the oven.

Very nice with butter, jam, and cream for afternoon tea.

JAMS & MARMALADES

Seville Orange Marmalade

Seville Orange Marmalade

INGREDIENTS

Makes 10 pint jars

> 1.5kg (3.3 lb) Seville oranges
> Juice of 2 lemons
> 3.5l (3¾ qt) water
> 2.75kg (13¾ cups) sugar

METHOD

1. Wash the fruit, cut it into halves and squeeze out the juice and pips (segments).
2. Slice the peel thinly and put it in a large pan with the fruit juices and water. Simmer gently for about 2 hours until the peel is really soft and the liquid is reduced by about half.
3. Remove from heat, add the sugar and stir until it has dissolved.
4. Return to the heat and boil rapidly until setting point is reached-about 15 minutes.
5. Leave to stand for about 15 minutes and then pot and cover in the usual way.

Lemon Curd

INGREDIENTS

Makes 1 jar

180g (1 cup) sugar
90g (6 Tbsp) butter
3 eggs
Zest and juice of 2 lemons

METHOD

1. Warm the butter in a saucepan.
2. Add the other ingredients.
3. Cook slowly, stirring continuously until the mixture thickens.
4. Remove, transfer to a jar, and store in a cool place until required.

Oxford Marmalade

Tip: Heat the jars in a very cool oven, 110°C (230°F), Gas mark ¼, before filling.

INGREDIENTS

Makes 7 pint jars

> 900g (2 lb) Seville oranges
> 1 lemon
> 2.25l (2¼ qt) water
> 1.8kg (9 cups) granulated or preserving sugar

METHOD

1. Line a sieve with a square of muslin (or a well-boiled handkerchief) and set it over a bowl.
2. Cut the oranges and lemon in halves, squeeze out the juice and strain it into the bowl.
3. Using a tsp, scoop out the pips and ragged pieces of pith into the sieve.
4. Tie up the muslin into a bag and put it in the preserving pan with the juice.
5. Cut the orange and lemon peel into short thick strips and add them to the pan with the water.
6. Bring to the boil, reduce the heat and simmer gently until the peel is very tender and the liquid is well reduced. This usually takes at least two hours.
7. Lift the muslin bag out of the liquid and squeeze as much as possible of its juice back into the pan.
8. Now add the sugar and stir the mixture on a low heat until the sugar has dissolved completely.
9. Simmer the marmalade slowly for about 1½ hours, or until it is dark in colour and has reached setting point. To test whether setting point has been reached, drop a little of the marmalade on to a cold plate. If it stiffens and forms a skin almost immediately, it will set.
10. Remove the pan from the heat and skim immediately.
11. Allow the marmalade to cool a little before stirring well and potting.

Cumberland Sauce

INGREDIENTS

Serves 12

225g (¾ cup) redcurrant jelly
90g (⅓ cup) port
Grated rind and juice of 1 lemon
Grated rind and juice of 1 large orange
Pinch of made mustard (prepared mustard)

METHOD

1. Bring the jelly and wine to the boil and simmer until it is reduced by a quarter.
2. Then add the other ingredients. Bring to the boil.
3. Serve separately with ham, cold meats, etc.

VEGETARIAN

Layered Pancakes with Spinach

Layered Pancakes with Spinach

INGREDIENTS
Serves 4-6

Pancake Batter
125g (1 cup) wholemeal (wholewheat) flour
1 egg beaten
300ml (1¼ cups) whole milk
15ml (1 Tbsp) oil

Filling
750g (1½ lb) spinach
Salt and pepper
227g (1 cup) cottage cheese
1 egg, beaten
Grated nutmeg

Finish
75g (⅔ cup) cheddar, cheese grated

METHOD

1. Place the flour in a bowl and make a well in the centre. Add the eggs, then gradually stir in half of the milk and the oil. Beat thoroughly until smooth. Add the remaining milk.
2. Heat a 15cm (6 inch) omelette pan and add a few drops of oil. Pour in 1 Tbsp of the batter and tilt the pan to coat the bottom evenly. Cook until the underside is brown, then turn over and cook for a further 10 seconds.
3. Turn onto a warmed plate. Repeat with the remaining batter making 12 pancakes. Stack interleaved with greaseproof paper as they are cooked. Keep warm.
4. Cook the spinach in a large pan with just the water clinging to the leaves after washing and a pinch of salt for 5 minutes.
5. Drain thoroughly. Chop finely and put in a bowl. Add the cottage cheese, egg, salt, black pepper, and nutmeg to taste. Mix thoroughly.

Layered Pancakes with Spinach

CONTINUED

6. Place a pancake on a heat proof plate, spread with some of the filling and cover with another pancake. Continue layering in this way, finishing with a pancake.

7. Sprinkle with the cheese and cook in a pre-heated moderately hot oven, 190°C (375°F), Gas Mark 5, for 30-40 minutes. Serve immediately as a main dish.

The cheddar cheese can be mature (sharp) cheddar.

Cauliflower Cheese Flan

INGREDIENTS
Serves 4-6

225g (½ lb) cauliflower florets
225ml (1 cup) whole milk
3 eggs
100g (1 cup) cheddar cheese, finely grated, divided
Salt and freshly ground pepper

Pastry
175g (1½ cups) plain flour
Pinch of salt
75g (⅓ cup) butter
30ml (2 Tbsp) cold water

Garnish
Tomato slices

METHOD

1. Heat the oven to 200°C (400°F), Gas mark 6. Place cauliflower florets in a large saucepan and just cover with cold water. Bring to the boil and boil for 5 minutes. Drain, rinse well under cold water, then drain again very thoroughly and pat dry.
2. On a lightly floured surface, roll out the pastry and use to line a 20cm (8 inch) plain flan ring on a baking sheet.
3. Arrange the cauliflower stalks downwards in the pastry-lined flan ring. In a bowl whisk together the milk and eggs and 75g (¾ cup) cheese. Season to taste with salt and pepper and pour it over the cauliflower. Sprinkle evenly with remaining grated cheddar cheese.
4. Cook in the oven for 40-45 minutes until the filling has only just set. Remove from the oven, leave to cool slightly, then carefully remove the flan ring and slide the flan on to a plate. Serve at once, garnished with the tomato slices.

Vegetable Soufflé

INGREDIENTS

Serves 4-6

900g (2 lb) mixed root vegetables, cooked and diced
75g (⅓ cup) pearl barley, soaked and then cooked
450ml (2 cups) fresh milk, divided
450g (1 lb) courgettes (zucchini), peeled and diced
Vegetable stock cube
Salt and freshly ground black pepper
Ground nutmeg – large pinch
3 large eggs, separated

METHOD

1. Place vegetables with barley in base of deep 1 litre (2pt) greased ovenproof dish. Dissolve stock cube in 150ml (⅔ cup) warm milk. Pour over vegetables.
2. Gently simmer courgettes (zucchini) in remaining milk with seasoning and nutmeg until soft. Purée in food processor or blender.
3. Beat egg yolks into courgette (zucchini) purée. Whisk whites until stiff and fold into purée. Pile on top of vegetables and bake at 190°C (375°F), Gas Mark 5, for 40 minutes until risen and golden. Serve immediately.

Potatoes, swede (rutabaga), and carrots are a tasty combination.

Broccoli Roulade

INGREDIENTS

Serves 4-6

Roulade
225g (½ lb) broccoli florets
40g (3 Tbsp) butter
25g (3½ Tbsp) wholewheat flour
150ml (⅔ cup) whole milk
3 eggs, separated
Salt and pepper

Tomato Sauce Filling
2 carrots
1 small onions
2 sticks celery
50g (¼ cup) butter
50g (½ cup) flour
50g (¼ cup) tomato paste
473ml (2 cups) white stock
Half clove of garlic
Bouquet garni (herbs tied together with string or in cheesecloth—use parsley, thyme, and bay leaf plus whatever other herbs are available.)
10g (1 Tbsp) sugar
5ml (1 tsp) vinegar
Salt and pepper to season

METHOD

Roulade
1. Steam broccoli lightly for 4-5 minutes. Chop up finely.
2. Melt butter. Stir in the flour and cook over low heat for 2 minutes. Add the milk and bring to boiling point, stirring well to avoid lumps. Simmer for 2-3 minutes.
3. Preheat the oven to Gas Mark 5 or 190°C (375°F). Line a 33 x 23cm (13 x 9 inch) Swiss roll tin with greaseproof paper.
4. Take the pan off the heat. Cool for 2 minutes and beat the egg yolks into the sauce, one at a time. Season well and add in chopped broccoli.

Broccoli Roulade

CONTINUED

5. Whisk the egg whites until stiff but not dry and gently fold them into the broccoli mix.
6. Spread this over the prepared Swiss roll tin and bake for 17-20 minutes.
7. Turn out onto a clean tea towel covered with a fresh sheet of greaseproof paper. Peel off the old sheet. Spread the filling over the roulade and roll. Place in fridge until set.

Tomato Sauce Filling

1. Dice carrots, onions, and celery in ½ inch pieces. Fry to a light golden brown in butter.
2. Add the flour. Mix to a roux and cook on the side of the stove to a sandy texture.
3. Add the tomato paste and mix well.
4. Gradually work in the boiling stock while stirring briskly to avoid lumps.
5. Add the crushed garlic and bouquet garni. Cover with a lid and simmer for 1½ hours.
6. Pass through a strainer into a clean saucepan.
7. Add the sugar and vinegar.
8. Correct the seasoning, colour, and consistency.

You may use a tomato sauce from the store, but fresh made is best and the consistency is thicker.

Vegetarian Vegetable Curry

INGREDIENTS
Serves 4-6

60ml (¼ cup) oil
2 onions, sliced
10ml (2 tsp) ground coriander
10ml (2 tsp) ground turmeric
15ml (1 Tbsp) curry powder
10ml (2 tsp) chopped root ginger
2 cloves garlic, crushed
4 carrots, sliced
350g (1½ cups) courgettes (zucchini), sliced
300ml (1⅓ cups) vegetarian stock
1 medium cauliflower
50g (½ cup) roasted cashew nuts
150g (⅔ cup) natural yogurt
Salt and pepper

METHOD

1. Heat the oil in a large pan. Add the onions and fry until softened.
2. Add the spices and garlic and cook for a further minute. Add the carrots and courgettes and fry for 2-3 minutes, stirring. Add the stock and the salt and pepper to taste.
3. Cover and simmer for 10-15 minutes. Break the cauliflower into florets. Add to the other vegetables and cook for a further 10 minutes.
4. Stir in the nuts and yogurt and heat through gently. Serve with brown rice as a main dish and accompaniments.

If you suffer from a nut allergy there is no need to add the cashew nuts.

Cheddar Cheese Pudding

INGREDIENTS

Serves 4-6

> 225g (2 cups) grated English mature cheddar cheese, divided
> 50g (½ cup) chopped roasted peanuts
> 8 slices wholemeal (wholewheat) bread
> 25g (2 Tbsp) butter
> 15ml (1 Tbsp) chopped fresh parsley
> 3 large eggs
> 450ml (2 cups) fresh whole milk
> 5ml (1 tsp) wholegrain mustard
> Salt and freshly ground black pepper

METHOD

1. Mix 100g (1 cup) cheese with the nuts and use to make sandwiches with the bread and butter. (Butter the bread, then make the sandwiches.) Cut into triangles. Arrange in a greased 1.1 litre (2 pt) ovenproof dish. Sprinkle with the remaining cheese and parsley.

2. Whisk eggs, milk, mustard, and seasoning. Pour over bread and leave to stand for 30 minutes.

3. Bake at 180°C (350°F), Gas Mark 4, for 40-45 minutes until set and golden.

Peanuts are optional.
Serve with grilled tomatoes.

Mushroom Crumble

INGREDIENTS

Serves 4-6

450g (1 lb) sliced mushrooms
100g (½ cup) butter, divided
175g (1½ cups) wholemeal (wholewheat) flour, divided
450ml (2 cups) fresh milk
100g (¾ cup) chopped fine onions
4 sliced leeks
10ml (1 Tbsp) chopped fresh parsley
5ml (1tsp) paprika
5ml (1tsp) mustard powder
75g (⅔ cup) grated mature English Cheddar Cheese
25g (3 Tbsp) porridge oats
Salt and black pepper

METHOD

1. Fry mushrooms, leeks, and onions in 50g (4 Tbsp) butter. Cook until soft. Add 50g (½ cup) flour. Gradually stir in milk. Season. Heat, stirring until sauce boils. Cover and simmer for 10 minutes. Add parsley, cook for 5 minutes. Pour into a greased, shallow, ovenproof dish.
2. Rub remaining butter and flour together. Add mustard, paprika, cheese, and oats. Sprinkle over the mushrooms, onions, and leeks.
3. Bake at 200°C (400°F), Gas Mark 6, for 25 minutes or until golden brown.

Vegetable and Nut Cobbler

INGREDIENTS

Serves 4-6

115g (½ cup) butter, divided
350g (3 cups) cauliflower florets
6 baby onions
175g (1½ cups) sliced carrots
150g (1¼ cups) sliced parsnips
175g (1½ cups) sliced green beans
397g (1 lb) can drained butter beans
568ml (2½ cups) fresh milk, divided
Black pepper
Vegetable stock cube
225g (2 cups) wholemeal (wholewheat) self-raising flour
10ml (2 tsp) baking power
50g (½ cup) walnut pieces
100g (1 cup) grated Red Leicester cheese

METHOD

1. Melt 15g (¼ cup) butter in large saucepan. Add vegetables (except butter beans), cover and cook gently for 10 minutes.

2. Add butter beans, stock cube, and 450ml (2 cups) milk. Transfer to a casserole dish. Cover and bake at 220°C (425°F), Gas Mark 7, for 15 minutes.

3. Sift flour and baking powder. Rub in remaining butter and add nuts. Stir in remaining milk and mix to a soft dough. Roll out to 1cm (½ inch) thick. Cut into 12 scones.

4. Remove casserole from oven. Sprinkle with cheese and arrange scones on top. Brush with milk. Bake at 180°C (350°F), Gas Mark 4, for 15 minutes until golden.

This is very nice made with Blue Stilton and cashew nuts instead of walnuts and Red Leicester cheese.

Stuffed Aubergines (Eggplant)

INGREDIENTS

Serves 4-6

2 aubergines (eggplants), halved lengthways
1 peeled and diced parsnip
1 peeled and diced carrot
2 diced courgettes (zucchini)
40g (3 Tbsp) butter, divided
Salt and freshly ground black pepper
5ml (1 tsp) mixed herbs
15ml (1 Tbsp) tomato paste
50g (⅓ cup) brown rice, cooked
215g (1 cup) can drained aduki beans (small, red beans)
25g (3 Tbsp) plain flour
568ml (2½ cups) fresh milk
100g (1 cup) mozzarella cheese

METHOD

1. Simmer aubergine halves gently in water for 3 minutes. Drain and cool. Scoop out flesh. Reserve casings.

2. Gently fry remaining vegetables in 25g (2 Tbsp) butter until soft. Season and stir in mixed herbs, tomato paste, aubergine, rice, and beans. Spoon into cases. Place in an ovenproof dish.

3. Place flour, remaining butter, and milk in a saucepan. Heat, stirring until the sauce boils. Cook for 2 minutes. Remove from heat. Season and add cheese, stirring until cheese melts. Pour over aubergines. Cover and cook at 190°C (375°F), Gas Mark 5, for 30 minutes.

Mature English Cheddar Cheese can be used in place of Mozzarella.

Lentil Rissoles (Small Croquettes)

INGREDIENTS
Serves 4-6

30ml (2 Tbsp) oil
1 onion, chopped
2 carrots, chopped
2 celery sticks, chopped
250g (1⅓ cups) lentils
600ml (2 cups) water
5ml (1 tsp) ground coriander
Salt and pepper
30ml (2 Tbsp) chopped parsley
175g (1½ cups) wholemeal
 (wholewheat) breadcrumbs
30ml (¼ cup) flour
1 egg, beaten
Oil for shallow frying

Yogurt Sauce
300g (1¼ cups) natural
 yogurt
15ml (1 Tbsp) chopped
 parsley
1 clove garlic, crushed

METHOD

1. Heat the oil in a pan. Add the onion, celery, and carrots, and fry until softened. Add the lentils, water, coriander, salt, and pepper to taste. Bring to the boil. Cover, reduce the temperature, and simmer for 50 minutes to 1 hour, stirring occasionally. Mix in the parsley and one third of the breadcrumbs. Turn onto a plate to cool.

2. Using floured hands, shape the mixture into rissoles (small croquettes) and coat with the flour. Dip into the beaten egg and coat with the remaining breadcrumbs.

3. Pour the oil into a frying pan to a depth of 5mm (¼ inch) and place over moderate heat. When hot, add the rissoles and fry until crisp and golden brown, turning once or twice.

4. To make the sauce, mix the yogurt, parsley, and garlic together. Serve the rissoles with the sauce in a sauce boat.

Vegetable Pie

INGREDIENTS

Serves 4

> 1kg (2.2 lb) mixed vegetables (carrots, peas, runner beans, cauliflower, etc.)
> 570ml (2 cups) white stock from the vegetables
> 110g (¼ lb) mushrooms
> 40g (4 Tbsp) butter, divided
> 3 or 4 tomatoes
> 40g (5 Tbsp) flour
> Salt and pepper
> 150ml (⅔ cup) fresh cream
> 110g (1 cup) grated cheese, divided
> Breadcrumbs

METHOD

1. Parboil the vegetables and strain, reserving the stock. Cut the vegetables up to a medium dice. Cook the mushrooms for 5 minutes in 1 Tbsp melted butter. Add to the other vegetables, together with the skinned tomatoes, chopped up. Place in a casserole dish.

2. Make the sauce by melting the rest of the butter, stir in the flour, salt, and pepper, and add vegetable stock and cream a little at a time. Bring to the boil, beating the sauce all the time to keep it smooth and glossy. Pour the sauce over the vegetables, and sprinkle with half of the cheese.

3. Sprinkle the top with breadcrumbs and the rest of the cheese. Bake in a moderate oven, 180°C (350°F), Gas mark 4, for 40-50 minutes, or until the top is golden brown.

DINING ETIQUETTE

FROM KITCHEN TO HIGH TABLE
DINING ETIQUETTE

By David Woodfine
    High Steward, Harris Manchester College,
    University of Oxford and

Karol Lahrman
    Social and Interpersonal Programming,
    O'More College of Design

DINING ETIQUETTE

Proper table manners and settings are not just for social situation, but should be a natural part of your daily life with family, friends, and in business. The knowledge and application of this art form will express your self-confidence in a variety of social settings. Dining is not simply nourishment for the body, it is an artistic setting for an elegant social affair. A key point to remember: the host or hostess is your guide for the evening, if you follow his or her lead you will be a great dinner guest. If, however, you are the host or hostess, we encourage you to continue reading as we lay out a plan for providing a memorable dining experience for you and your guests.

BEFORE DINNER

Prior to dinner, cocktails and appetizers may be offered, allowing guests to socialize with one another. Pre-dinner cocktails may be offered outside or inside.

ANNOUNCING DINNER

The announcement of dinner can come in different forms.

- The host or hostess of a smaller dinner may walk among guests announcing "dinner is served" and guide the guests to the dining room.
- Household staff may inform the guests with an announcement asking them to proceed to the dining room.
- The host of larger parties may dim the lights to inform the guests to move into the banquet room.

Guests will then gather around the dinner table where their names have been written on place cards, or they will wait for the host or hostess to assign their seats. Only when the host or hostess sits, are the guests to sit.

SEATING

Place cards are arranged by the host to allow guests to share commonalities in conversation. Traditionally, guests are seated as male, female, male, female, etc., separating couples.

To switch or rearrange place cards is considered poor etiquette. At the conclusion of the dinner, guests may use the cards to record the names and the contact information of the other guests, if desired.

If the dinner is provided by a hosting couple, one will be seated at one end of the table and the other at the opposite end of the table.

If there are guests of honor in attendance, they should be placed to the right of the host and/or hostess.

The male guest of honor sits on the hostess's right, the next important man sits on her left. The female guest of honor sits on the host's right, the second most important woman sits on the host's left.

The male guest of honor seats the woman on his right. The man sitting on the hostess's left seats the hostess.

Other gentlemen in the party help seat the lady to his right by pulling out her chair. Once she is seated, the man then takes the seat beside her.

OVERSIGHT OF A FORMAL DINNER

A formal dining affair is prepared by a chef and served by professional staff. The evening is overseen by a major-domo, or head or high steward, who makes sure the needs of all guests are met. Those who have risen to the level of a high steward have achieved a heightened degree of prestige, honor, and trust. This individual makes arrangements and acts on behalf of the owner, the college, etc. The major-domo or high steward may also pour the wine at a formal dinner party and will observe that the services for the guests are being carried out as desired, though he often does so at a distance from behind the hostess.

SERVING

When a meal is comprised of three to six or more courses, the placement and clearance of plates at the table should scarely be noticed.

Various courses for a formal dinner may include the following:

Course One: cold starters, light appetizers, a variety of hors d'oeuvres, or soup.

Course Two: soup (if soup is not served as the first course), fish, salad (an American tradition to serve before the main course), bread, pasta (which may also be served as the main course in the form of spaghetti, lasagna, etc.).

Course Three: main course, which usually includes meat or fish (if fish is not a part of course two), along with vegetables.

Course Four: salad (a British tradition to serve after the main course).

Course Five: dessert, cheese (may be served before or after dessert), dessert wine.

Course Six: cheese, fruit, coffee, tea, port.

Appetizers and other types of hors d'oeuvres served before the guests sit down at the dining table, and items served after retiring from the dining table, are generally not counted as *a course*. Whether these items are offered as a part of the pre-dinner and post-dinner social experience, as a part of the formal sit-down dinner or not at all, is at the discretion of the host and hostess. Any of these choices is acceptable.

The ratio of servers to guests depends on the number of courses, and the serving requirements for each course. To serve each course at its proper temperature it is suggested one server for four to six guests. If sauce is a part of the meal, two servers work as a team, one to serve the course and the second to offer the sauce.

To keep fingers from the rim of the plate, the server holds a fresh plate in the palm of his left hand and slides it into place. The server's fingers are not to touch plates that hold food, although the server's fingers may touch the rim of the plate while clearing. Plates are served and cleared from the left side. The server's right hand clears a used plate, and the left hand places a fresh plate. This way there is never an empty space before the guest.

Exceptions:

- To expedite service of the first course, the server may carry two plates to the table at one time.
- After the table is crumbed, the server may carry two dessert plates to the dining room at one time.
- Drinks are served and cleared from the right side only.

To promote an atmosphere that is conducive to conversation by the guests, a server should enter and exit the dining room only to set a plate before each guest; to serve the course; to present sauce, if needed; to serve wine; to replenish water as needed; and to clear the plate.

The water goblet and wine glasses remain on the table throughout the meal. When the same wine is offered with consecutive courses, it is served in the same glass. Only the sherry glass is removed at the end of the course it accompanies. If a guest informs the server they prefer a non-alcoholic beverage, the server may remove the wine glasses.

ORDER OF SERVICE

Traditionally, the host and hostess were served first, to demonstrate that the food was not poisoned.

The custom today is for the honored guest to be served first, starting with the female guest of honor who is seated on the host's right. Servers move around the table counterclockwise from her, serving the host last.

Beverage service progresses clockwise. When a formal affair has no guest of honor, service begins with the most important female guest, ladies served first.

NAPKIN ETIQUETTE

In setting the table, the napkin is placed to the left of the plate and forks, or in the center of the plate. Prior to placing the napkin in your lap, wait for the host or hostess to take his or her napkin off the table and place it in his or her lap. Then unfold your napkin in one smooth motion, placing it in your lap, with the fold against your body. Use your napkin often during the meal to blot or pat your lips. If wearing lipstick, blot your lips before taking a drink of your beverage.

When leaving the table temporarily:

- Place the napkin on your chair.
- If the chair is upholstered, place the napkin soiled side up.

At the meal's end:

- The napkin is loosely folded at the end of the meal.
- If a plate is in the center of your place setting, when leaving the table lay the napkin to the left or right of the plate.
- If the center of your place setting is empty, the napkin is laid in the middle of the place setting.
- Leave your napkin in loose folds that keep soiled parts hidden.
- If coffee is served at the table after the meal, the napkin remains in the lap.

Do not wipe cutlery or glassware with your napkin, and do not tuck a napkin into your collar.

A napkin should never be returned to the table before the meal has ended.

UTENSIL ETIQUETTE

The place settings used depend on the type of meal being served and the style of dining event. The utensils are placed in order of use from the outside in, with the forks to the left of the plate, knives and spoons to the right.

During the meal, it is acceptable to use both British style (tines down) for meat and American style (tines up) for side dishes.

British Style (fork tines down)

- Hold your fork in your left hand, tines downward with the index finger touching the neck of the handle.

- Hold your knife in your right hand low to the plate. Extend your index finger along the top of the blade. The knife is used during the meal to cut and carry food to the fork.

- Cut three to four bits of food at a time. The knife is kept in the right hand or placed across the plate as the other hand moves the fork to your mouth.

- The English do not switch knives and forks. The knife remains in the right hand, and the fork remains in the left during the meal.

- If your knife is not needed, it remains on the table.

American Style (fork tines up)

- When not using a knife, hold your fork in the right hand like a pencil, with the shank extended between your thumb and second and third fingers. Your fourth and fifth fingers rest in your hand. The index finger is extended along the top of the fork.

- When using a knife to cut food, hold your knife in the right hand with the handle cupped in the palm of your hand, along with your third, fourth, and fifth fingers. Your index finger is placed on the back of the blade. Your thumb is held against the side of the handle.
- When using a knife to cut food, hold your fork in the left hand much like in British Style above—tines downward with the index finger touching the neck of the handle.
- Three to four bites of food should be cut, then place the knife on the edge of the plate. You may then switch the fork from the left hand to the right with tines facing up as noted above, then move the food to your mouth.

Temporary Placement of Utensils

The placement of utensils during and after the meal is part of the art of dining. There are two recommeneded resting positions for temporary placement of the fork and knife during dinner conversations or while sipping from a glass, so the server will realize that you are not ready for your plate to be removed.

British Style
- The fork is laid on the side of the plate with the tines turned downward and the handle in the eight o'clock position.

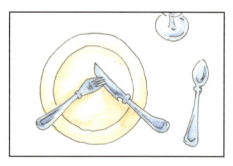

- The knife handle is placed in the four o'clock position. creating an inverted V (slightly angled) fork tines resting over the blade of the knife.

American Style

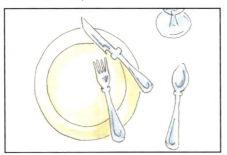

- The knife is rested on the top right rim of the plate.
- The fork is laid near the knife with the fork tines upward.

Using Two Utensils

In formal dining, two utensils are used with the appetizer course, salad course, main course, dessert course, and fruit course.

Soup Spoons

If soup or dessert is served in a deep bowl, a stemmed bowl, or a cup set on a plate, place your utensil(s) on the under-plate when finished. If the under-plate is too small to balance the spoon, the spoon is laid in the bowl. If the bowl is a soup plate (shallow and wide), leave the spoon in the bowl.

Utensil Placement when Finished with a Course

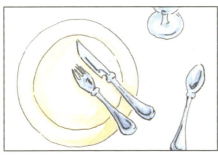

- Place the knife and fork parallel with the handles in the four o'clock position on the right edge of the plate. The knife should be outside and the fork inside.
- The tips should rest in the well of the plate in the ten o'clock position, blades down.
- This position signals the server that you are finished.

Miscellaneous Utensil Etiquette
- If silverware is dropped in the floor ask for a replacement. Do not bend down to retrieve the item.
- Never place any utensil that has been used directly on the table. Instead, place it diagonally on the edge of your plate.
- Never rest a utensil half on a plate and half on the table.

CLEARING OF THE TABLE

Formal dining servers clear the plates only after the majority of guests are finished. They carry plates to the kitchen one at a time or quietly place them on a tray at the side of the room. Plates are removed to the left side of the guests.

To clean the table before dessert, the removing of crumbs may take place. The server stands to the left of each guest and brushes the crumbs onto a small plate or tray.

Before serving dessert, the table should be cleared of items unrelated to the dessert course, starting with the largest items, like plates and stemware, then working to the smallest items, like flatware. Large articles may be cleared one in each hand. Smaller items are cleared on a small tray.

AFTER DINNER

After dinner and dessert are completed, the guests may retire from the dinner table for port, brandy, cigars, coffee, tea, etc. The ladies often retire to a drawing room, sitting room, or lady's parlor, and the gentlemen remain at the dining table or move to a special room such as a pool room, library, or gentleman's parlor. The ladies and gentlmen may also retire to the same room or space for after dinner socializing.

THE ART OF DINING

Guests should take their hints from the hostess in all things. Fine dining has been noted by many chefs and lovers of the culinary arts as similar to performing a beautiful piece of music. It is art in motion. The musicians, the dining guests, begin with the outside utensils and work their way in on both sides. The conductor is the host or hostess who picks up the first utensil, and the musical masterpiece is set in motion.

- Sit up straight in your chair.
- Match your eating pace with that of the dinner guests and hostess.
- Taste your food prior to adding spices of salt and pepper.
- Pass rolls or condiments to the right and initiate passing even if you do not take any.
- When food is placed directly in front of you, offer it to the guests on each side of you prior to serving yourself, then pass the item to your right.
- Soup should be served already in the bowl. Spoon soup away from you, tilting the bowl away from you if necessary.
- Be courteous in the dinner conversation and when speaking about the food. Respect the other guests.
- Do not stack your plates or push dishes away from you.

USE OF A FINGER BOWL

After the main course, the server may deliver a finger bowl, allowing guests to cleanse their hands prior to dessert being served. Finger bowls hold warm water, and may be served on a small plate.

- Dip fingers into water, one hand at a time.
- You may touch wet fingers lightly to your lips, if desired, for cleaning.
- Dry your fingers and lips with the napkin.
- Move the bowl to one side of your plate.

THE FORMAL TABLE SETTING

As a general rule, when preparing a formal place setting, everything should be geometrically placed. The centerpiece sits at the center of the table and the place settings all sit at equal distances. You may add other flower arrangements or decorations. At a formal dinner, the space in front of the guests must always hold a plate, therefore, service plates are placed on the table before the guests enter to dine.

Another general rule for any table setting is to include no more than three utensils on either side of the dinner plate at any one time. The exception is the oyster (or seafood) fork, which may be

placed to the right of the last spoon. This is the only fork to be placed on the right side of the plate. If more than three courses are served before dessert, the utensils for the remaining courses are to be brought in with the food. The initial table setting for a typical formal dinner should look something like what follows:

Placement of the Service Plate

The service plate or charger serves as an underplate for the plate holding the first course that will be brought to the table after guests are seated. The service plate will remain in place until the main course is served, at which time the two plates will be exchanged.

Bread and Butter Plates

When bread and butter are served, a small bread and butter plate is placed above the forks, to the left of the service plate.

Glasses
- Water glass: The water glass is placed above each guest's dinner knife, with the other dining glasses to the right of the water glass as follows below.
- Champagne glass: A champagne flute, if used, may be located between the water glass and the red wine glass, often pushed up and behind those two glasses.

- Red wine glass: A red wine glass has a wider globe and is placed to the right of the water glass.
- White wine glass: The glass with the longer stem and cylindrical globe is the white wine glass. The white wine glass is placed to the right of the red wine glass.
- Sherry glass: A small sherry glass also may be present to the right of the wine glasses. If so, the white wine glass may be pushed above the red wine glass, to the right of the champagne flute.

Forks
- Salad fork: Place the salad folk directly to the plate's left, one inch from the plate. (When serving salad before the main course, place the salad fork to the left of the dinner fork.)
- Dinner fork: Place the dinner fork to the left of the salad fork.
- Fish fork (if used): Place the fish fork to the left of the dinner fork.
- Seafood fork or oyster fork (if used): Place the seafood fork to the right of the soup or fruit spoon. It may also be laid next to the soup spoon in a parallel position.

Knives
- Dinner knife: Place the dinner or meat fork directly to the right of the plate, one inch from the plate.
- Fish knife: Place the fish knife to the right of the dinner knife.
- Butter knife: Place the butter knife on the butter plate, diagonally with the handle toward the guest.
- Knife blades are always placed with cutting edge toward the plate.

Spoons
- Soup spoon or fruit spoon: place directly to the right of the knives.

Dessert Spoons and Forks
- Dessert fork and spoon: place horizontally above the dinner plate.

Salt and Pepper Shakers
- The salt and pepper shakers are placed between two place settings.
- The salt shaker is placed to the right of the pepper shaker.
- The pepper shaker is placed to the left of and slightly above the salt shaker.

DINING ETIQUETTE REFERENCES

In addition to the authors' years of experience, the following sources were referenced to provide balance and consistency between the dining customs of the British and Americans. Both websites are excellent resources for additional research on proper dining etiquette.

"Formal Dining." British Culture, British Customs and British Traditions. Learn English Network. 2012. Web.15 March 2012. < http://www.learnenglish.de/culture/eatingculture.htm#Table>

Lininger, Mike. "Formal Dining Service." Etiquette Scholar.n.p. 2011. Web. 15 March 2012 <http://www.etiquettescholar.com/dining_etiquette/table_manners/serving_techniques/formal_dinner_service.html>

CPSIA information can be obtained at www.ICGtesting.com
Printed in the USA
LVIW01n0806210415
435131LV00001B/2